ALSO BY DHEEP MATHARU

A NEW YORK KIND OF LOVE, VOLUME 1

A NEW YORK KIND OF LOVE, VOLUME 2

A NEW YORK KIND OF LOVE, VOLUME 3

A NEW YORK KIND OF LOVE, VOLUME 4

A NEW YORK KIND OF LOVE, VOLUME 5

A NEW YORK KIND OF LOVE, VOLUME 6

A NEW YORK KIND OF LOVE, VOLUME 7

A NEW YORK KIND OF LOVE, VOLUME 8

ON THE FENCE, VOLUME 1

ON THE FENCE, VOLUME 2

ON THE FENCE, VOLUME 3

ON THE FENCE, VOLUME 4

ON THE FENCE, VOLUME 5

A NEW YORK KIND OF LOVE

Volume One

My Secret Journal of a Coke Addict

Dheep Matharu

Bestselling Author of *A New York Kind of Love*

This work is a memoir. It reflects the author's present recollections of her experiences. Certain names, locations, and identifying characteristics have been changed, and certain individuals are composites. Dialogue and events have been recreated from memory and, in some cases, have been compressed to convey the substance of what was said or what occurred.

Published by Dheep Matharu
Copyright 2018 © Dheep Matharu

All rights reserved. No part of this book may be reproduced or transmitted in any form or by any means, electronic or mechanical, including photocopying, recording, or by any information storage and retrieval system without written permission of the publisher, except for the inclusion of brief quotations in a review.

Tradepaper ISBN: 978-1-976985-99-7
Digital ISBN: 978-1-976985-99-4

SPECIAL INVITATION

Be sure to grab a free sample of my prequel memoir series *On the Fence*, available on Amazon worldwide:

DHEEPMATHARU.COM/ONTHEFENCE

You can connect with me personally on Facebook.com/DheepUncensored and Instagram @DheepMatharu. Thank you for allowing me to share my personal stories with you. I pray my books move you. Amen.

Dheep Matharu is a new age Christian spiritualist, life coach and author of two popular memoir series, On the Fence and the bestselling A New York Kind of Love. Having, spent nearly three years living in New York City within a corporate career, she now resides in her hometown of Kent, England.

Chapter One: Instagram

Friday morning, 3am

Everyone has left.

JJ just left to meet her Tinder hook-up.
Fi and the rest of her crew left an hour ago for an afterparty, at her restaurant in the Upper East Side.

And here I am.
Snorting Charlie.

On my lonesome.

☐ About Charlie ☐

Meet 'Charlie'.

He's our best friend.
You may hear us saying things like…

"Are we seeing Charlie tonight?"
"Is Charlie with you tonight?"
"I can't, sorry… I have a date with Charlie."

Tonight, Charlie is taking me on a trip down memory lane.

He's showing me half-naked photos of my ex and his new flame on Instagram.

They've just come back from Cancun.

Sitting on my couch at 3am

I'm getting kind of tired of this game.
Every day is shittier than the last.
And if I hear another rendition of Justin Bieber's 'What Do You Mean' I'm going to shoot myself in the face.

Tonight,

a guy
I just met
asked me
if I would

marry him.

Legit.

I'm **one hundred percent sure** that means he wants to get in my knickers.

Coincidentally…
that's also my cue
to tell him

to fuck right off.

Still, it was a welcomed change from the usual Thursday night banter:

"Come to my hotel room."

"Come to my hotel room to do some Charlie."

"Come to my hotel room to FUCK and do some Charlie."

So, I thought, what the heck.
I said, "SURE, let's talk more on this tomorrow because I'm going home now."

"Can I come with you?" he said.

"No!"

So, then he disappeared, never to be seen again.

Now I'm kinda stalking this guy from Tinder.
That's why I'm still up at 3am instead of getting the beauty sleep I'm supposed to be.
I don't know how he found me.
I must have linked Instagram to my Tinder profile by mistake.

No-one can ever find me on Instagram.

That's why I only have TEN FOLLOWERS.

Instagram wasn't cool in London when I left for New York City.
It was something we used to share pictures of our food or make us look cute in pictures.
So we could add them to our Facebook posts.
It was only until I moved to New York City a year ago that suddenly EVERYONE was asking me questions like:

'What's your IG?',

'Add me on IG',

'Follow me and I'll follow you back'.

To which, I usually responded with something like:

"Sorry.

But what the fuck is my fucking 'I' 'G' .

And where do I find it?

Because you all seem to know more about it than I do…"

When I FIRST got Instagram, I didn't know what to do with it. So, I asked Facebook.

"What can I do on Instagram that I can't already do on Facebook. Discuss."

It was my most liked post of the year.

Here are just some of the replies:

"It's just cool."
"I like to see what the Kardashians are doing."
"Sometimes I share cool quotes with my friends."
"There's always fit girls on there."
"It's like reading the Sunday paper, everywhere you go."

Don't even get me STARTED on **Tinder**...

I've been playing Tinder all day long
and I've only won 3 games.

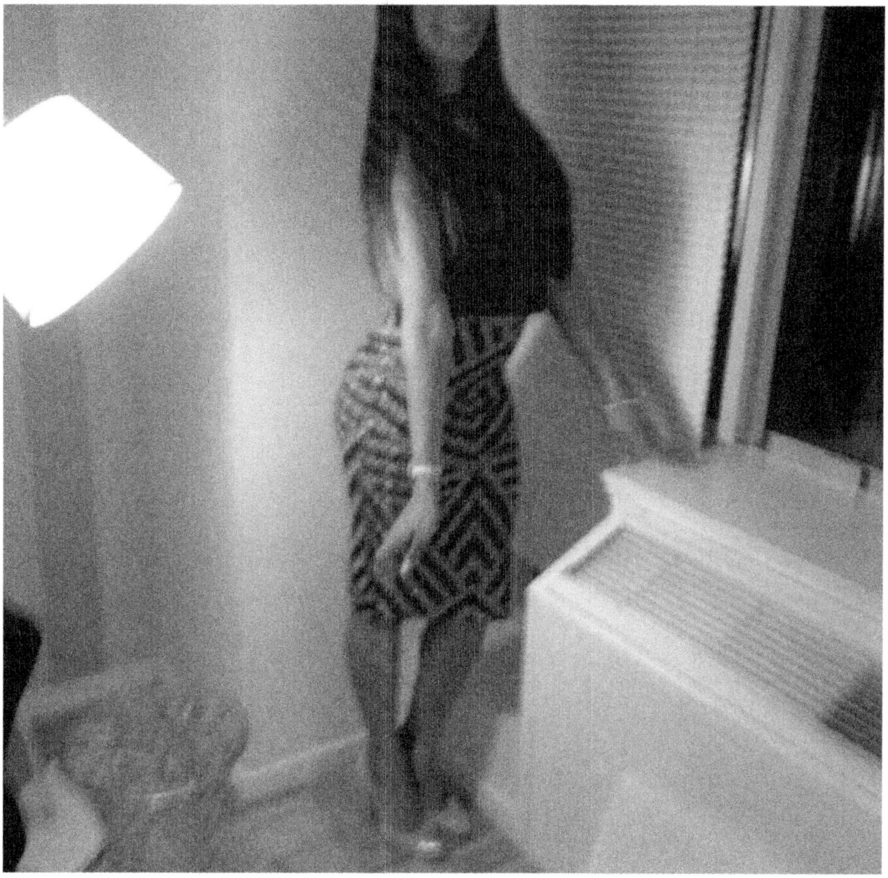

Playing on Tinder

The first guy messaged me and asked me,
'Do you want sex,
and do you want it now?'

The second one messaged me,
'Hi'
in the middle of the night
<u>and then by morning he had blocked me.</u>

By the time the third guy messaged me to say,
"I see you like coffee, I like coffee too."

I decided to quit.

I suppose I'm not much of a **gamer.**

Strangely, a few days after I deleted Tinder, I discovered I now had

<u>one new follower on Instagram.</u>

Mystery follower on Instagram

A David Beckham-esque silver fox.

He's not really a 'silver fox' **per se**.
He's just well over the age of twenty-five and has managed to grow an **adult beard.**
 - No, it's NOT a glued-on Santa Claus-esque beard, found in Chelsea.
 - And no, it's NOT paired with a glued on 'man bun' either.

So, on that basis, I'm going to assume that means he at least has his shit together.

#justsaying

His profile name is 'Mr E NYC'.

Mr E NYC??

Maybe he hasn't got his shit together after all.

He sounds like the local drug dealer, specialising in Ecstasy.

Still,
a good contact to have,
either way.

For argument's sake let's call him
'Mr E'.
Mr E was the most interesting person to start following me on Instagram.

He was also the only person that wasn't already my friend **in real life.**

The same friends who, thanks to Instagram and Facebook, now yell at me **TWICE** for not liking their posts.

"If you <u>saw</u> I was in Spain, why didn't you like <u>at least one</u> of my posts??"

That's why, when someone that I don't know starts following me I start to get a little 'inquisitive', shall we say.

That excludes:
- bots with names like 'Get 10,000 follows free'.
- or the 'follow-for follow' / 'like-for-like' clones.
- or anyone that is basically selling me porn.

I'm looking at his profile and I have to say, this MR E guy is pretty darn **FINE**.

Fine / Fit / Hellafine.

Translation:
Someone I'd like to fuck.

☐ About Mr E ☐

Mr E was not your typical Instagrammer.

One.
He probably had a great body, but he didn't need the whole world to see it.

Two.
He may <u>once</u> have had a great body, but he didn't need the whole world to see it.

Three.
He may <u>once</u> have had a great body, but he didn't need the whole world to see it… and he wasn't pretending <u>he still had it</u> today.

Even if he didn't.

Some fun facts about Mr E…

One.
He's a little vain, but that's okay…
Aren't we all.

Two.
Every photo is of HIM, or his DOG.

Three.
He seems to like filters… a LOT.

Four.
He seems to like filters… MORE THAN ME.

I see he does have some strong qualities as well…

One.
There are hardly any girls on his page.

So, it's hopefully safe to say he is not married or with girlfriend.

Two.
The only girls on his page appear to be **FAMILY**.

I know this because
    a) none of the girls are pouting,
    b) none of them have their breasts out, and
    c) all of them look like a female version of him.

Three.
He takes pictures of food.
But of the ingredients,
BEFORE it's cooked.

Which means he must be **good with his hands.**

Four.
He wears a suit 99.8% of the time.
This means he has a job.

Or at least he had a job at some point in his lifetime.

Five.
His mum comments on e-v-e-r-y picture.
With comments like, "My darling boy", "I love you son" or "I miss you".

Which reaffirms <u>point one</u> above, that he is not married or with girlfriend.
At least not on THIS PROFILE, with his mother watching.

But I'm still struggling with one thing.

Is he a drug dealer??

Reasons he might be a drug dealer:

One.
His name is 'Mr E NYC'.

Two.
He wears a suit 99.8% of the time.

Three.
The remaining 0.2% of the time he is pictured 'smoking blunts'.

Four.
On a few of his pictures are comments from followers like, "What do you actually DO for a living??"

Five.
To which he replies,
"I make paper with pictures of presidents on them."

Six.
Followed by several emojis of flying dollar bills.
☐☐☐☐☐☐☐

'I MAKE PAPER WITH PICTURES

OF PRESIDENTS ON THEM.'

He either actually does work in a paper factory

OR

he's selling drugs.

I JUST DON'T KNOW.

Back to sitting on the couch at 3am

I have work in 3 hours.
I haven't slept yet, but I need to think of a comment for Mr E's latest post.

He's wearing a watch.
It's big, gold and SPUNKY.
It fills the ENTIRE FRAME.
Do you think he might be loaded?

Clap. Clap. Clap.

Still, I'm reserving judgement…
Because there's something about him that I kinda like.

I'm about to throw my hat into the ring…

Mr E, I've been stalking you for months and you STILL haven't:
- Liked any of my photos.
- Commented on any of my photos.
- DM'd me.

It's time to pull out the big guns.
Something a) witty b) flirtatious and c) **fun.**

"I think I'd look better

on your arm @mr_e_nyc #drippingingold"

I'm a modern day, female Ricky Gervais.

The next day??...
Not feeling so clever.
I kinda wish I hadn't said anything.

I woke up 2 hours later and unlocked my phone.
Staring in front of me was **the stupidest** comment known to humankind.
Do you ever just wake up, enjoy a few seconds of blissful ignorance and then open your phone, to reveal the most fucking stupidest comment EVER?
You're wondering to yourself, "Who even wrote that?! I bet they're feeling like a dick today."
Merp.
YOU.

YOU WROTE IT, YOU DICK.

I feel really fucking stupid now.
Perfect.

NOTE TO SELF:
Ambien and Charlie DO NOT go well together.

It's a work day.
You don't have time for this shit.
Sober up, sober up.
Charlie, Charlie, Charlie.

At work and I stink of fags and booze.
I'm paranoid as FUCK, shaking like an electric toothbrush, avoiding any eye contact and stuffing my nose with tissues like the HOOVER DAM.
Bathroom.
Charlie, Charlie, Charlie.
I should have called in sick.
Then I'd be home, doing this.
Russian Roulette.
Spin.
Charlie or Ambien, or both.

"Psssst… Jen?… Jen??"

▫▫ **About Jen** ▫▫

Jen is my favourite person at work.

Jen is like a cup of tea on a rainy day.

She's like the mum I never had, but always wanted.
She looks like the pretty girl next door that never says a peep, but then always somehow gets the guy in the end.
Except, this is New York City, so **instead** she's single and 40, without even a hope of meeting a guy that isn't
already fucking the entire city.

And then some.

Jen is around my height, maybe a little shorter, so if I'm 5"7 then she's probably around 5"4 or 5"5.
She has dark brown hair cut in a neat, straight line skimming her shoulders.
It's perfectly straight, all the time.
Except some days when it's neatly curled, in equal and equidistant sections.

My hair is rarely brushed, let alone cleaned or straightened.
It's a war of curls vs waves and some straight sections, knotted and matted together at the base of my scalp and then

hung over the front of my right shoulder and dragged all the way down to my hips.

Sometimes it's black, sometimes it's brown and sometimes it's caramel, depending on the lighting.

I like it messy, sexy and ready to go.

The rare few times I manage to drag a brush though it, I feel like I should be in a music video.

So, I behave like an **idiot.**
A DIVA.

Jen is whiter than white.
If I'm allowed to say that.
Except in the summer when she has a barely noticeable tan.

My face is the colour of caramel, most hours of the day.
But whilst I'm sleeping, the colours are something like
a Mars bar,
a Snickers bar
and a Milky Way
all having a three-way…

On my face.

The rest of me is caramel
all year round.

Except in the summer months it can turn from CARAMEL to COFFEE in 0 to 30 seconds, in direct sunlight.

Back to Jen and the office place.

Three months into the new job, I discovered Jen.
Jen is the saving grace of this whole sordid ordeal.
She and I have been plotting the demise of the whole banking industry since DAY ONE in this team.
Neither of us has developed an affinity to Joan or Chloe - our boss and her lemming.
Neither has anyone else on the floor, but that's another story for another time.

"Jen, can you come and take a look at this please? … I need your help…"

Jen is my Bible on relationships.
I am the Guru, let me just clarify.
<u>But</u> she keeps me in check and makes sure I'm following protocol.

"Sure, what is it?" Jen replied.

"I need you to check that this comment isn't **borderline insanity**."

She shuffles over with her chair, wheeling it closer to mine.
She stares at the comment to Mr E, on my phone.
I can see her mouthing the words to herself over and over again.

She's probably wondering if
I've lost the plot.

"SO?" I said, losing my patience.

"It's…
Fine,"
she said.

IT'S.
NOT.
FINE,
IS IT JEN??

Jen was clearly not impressed.
She asked me why I didn't just go on Tinder or Bumble 'like the rest of us'.
But then, neither of us were expecting Mr E to respond to my comment that very day.

It was genius.
Poetic, almost…

"Let's try it on for size

@dheepmatharu"

HE'S MY SOULMATE.

He speaks my language.

He likes making sexy jokes about **watches**.

Enough said.

I figure I'm on a roll here, so I decide that DM'ing him is the best way to go:

"So where are you taking me for a drink?"

Wait, I have plans to meet Jono tonight...

"So where are you taking me for a drink tomorrow?"

Done.
Send.

He may like watches, **but he clearly doesn't know how to use one.**
Twenty-four hours later and I still had no response.

I refreshed Instagram almost one hundred times.

I restarted the app.

I restarted all the apps on my entire phone.

I restarted my phone.

I asked Jono to send me a message ON THE APP, just to be sure.

Everything was working fine.

In that time, however, Mr E, had
- posted **2 pictures**,
- responded to **3 comments**
- and liked **5 pictures**.

I flipped over to the profile of one of the pictures he'd liked:

@girl_wears_zero_clothing
992 Posts
2240 Followers
876 Following
NYC Fashion designer / stylist

I wonder what he must like about her?
She wears zero clothing, for a start.
And she has 2240 followers.
Bummer.

In her first picture I see her butt.
Wearing a thong.
Her butt is bigger than her face.

FACT.

In her second picture she is wearing a bra.
She has a six-pack.

**She has
a six-pack,
for Christ's sake.**

I stared at the half-eaten donut in my hand
and chomped another bite.

FFS.

I have 12 pictures on my Instagram.
They are of my best achievements.

One.
A paint-by-numbers I did and stayed within the lines.

Two.
The results of my Series 7 exam (87%).

Three.
Proof of me flipping my ponytail all the way around my head. Which took seven attempts, by the way.

Four & Five.
The time I met Pamela Andersen and the time I met Mr Brainwash.

And so forth.

Five weeks later, I add a new post of me in Tampa, FL, and Mr E suddenly replies.

"I'd love to take you out!! Are you in the city? Or playing in the water in Florida?"

I'm sure it had **nothing** to do with the picture I just posted
of me in a skimpy bikini,
straddling a jet ski.

And so, I was deeply moved by Mr E's response, as I'm sure you can guess.
So moved was I, that I wanted to fuck with him a little first.
I applied the Three-Day Rule.
I responded with a brief and succinct message:

"Back in the apple."

I capped it to 5 syllables.
Why?
New Yorkers have the attention span of a **gnat**.
He responded promptly, 2 days later:

"What are you doing gorgeous?"

To which I replied, also promptly 2 days later:

"Waiting for our date."

I didn't expect a response. In my experience with guys in New York, messages rarely progressed past this point.

However, to my complete surprise, he replied almost straight away.

"We are definitely going out!
I like a woman who knows what she wants!!!
What works best for you?
I don't even know your name!!
I should know your name, right?
Do you live in the city?"

Look at those exclamation marks, dripping all over the place!! This boy's got a lot to say.
He must know Charlie.

But he's still a chauvinistic pig, after my body and not my mind, so he hasn't won me over yet.
With deliberation, I coolly replied:

"I live in Chelsea."

There's no way he's going to reply to that...
But I kinda hope he will.

He replied the next morning:

> **"How's it going gorgeous?
> When would you like to meet?
> I'm Ethan btw."**

I might have replied but then Charlie took me on a 3-day bender.
So that was that.
Over the next week we exchanged a few more mundane messages, which I ended by sending him my phone number and left the ball in his court.

That way,
if he doesn't reply,
it's on him.

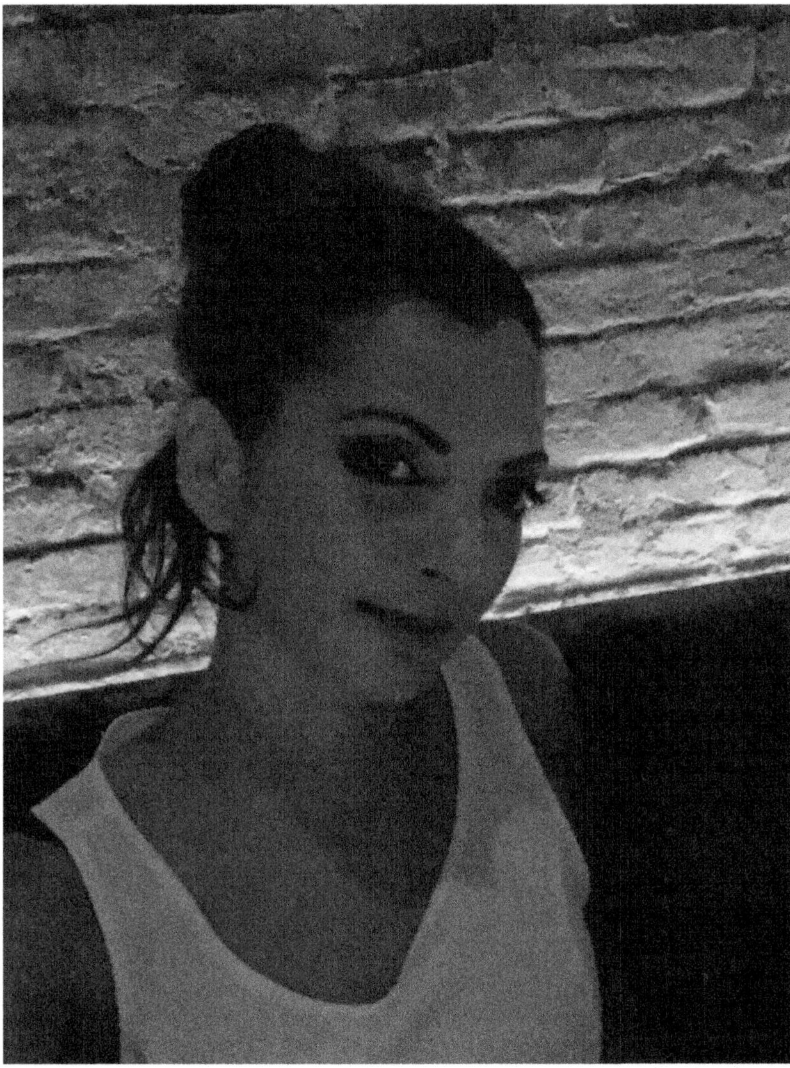

Chapter Two: Meeting

Someone is calling my phone

It's Fi…

About Fi

Fi is really, really tall.
She has to be over six foot,

**but no-one
really knows
for sure.**

She **looks** a lot like my sister,
and she **acts** a lot like my sister,

**except
she actually
likes me,**

which is probably why we're such good friends.

Fi has red hair.
Swearing features **heavily** in her vocabulary.
And she doesn't like it if you don't let her smoke and drink at the same time.

We have that in common.

Fi is from London but we met in New York, outside Mr Chow's.
She was smoking a cigarette.

And I needed a light.
I was also bored, waiting for the crew to arrive.

If it wasn't for all of the above, I probably **still** would have met Fi.

We were soulmates.
But the friends kind.

She **behaves** like she was raised on Perignon and Prada.

Except she truly isn't.

Fi, like me, hasn't lined her body or any part of it with silicone, collagen or any other plumpers.

Just Charlie and unlimited cigarettes.

We pay for our own clothes,
our own jewellery
and our own shoes…

Most of the time.

We pay for our own rent,
out of our own salaries.

Almost all the time.

Fi owns a restaurant,

which is the coolest thing in the world.

One day,
if I grow up,
I want to be

just
like
her.

One day.

The first day we met she took me to her friend's bar downtown,
    where we
    smoked cigarettes all night,
    stayed out until 4am
    and played with Charlie.

We talked shit about our hopes and dreams.
Planned how to take over the world.
Agreed how amazing we were
going to be.

One day.

I better answer my phone.

It's Fi…

"H-E-E-E-Y FI BABE!!"

"Hey babe! How you doing?"

"Good, good. Hungover. Usual."

"Good, good. Hey babe?"

"Yeah, what's up?"

"Remember my friend Zach?"

"Yeah?"

Who the fuck is Zach.

"Well his friend, Bailey, is driving his boat to Staten Island for the day."

"Yeah?…"

"Well he's invited me and you… You comin'?"

He doesn't even know me.

⬜⬜ "On his BOAT?"

"Yeah."

⬜⬜ "His B-O-A-T, babe?"

"Yeah, he's got a boat."

**Who the fuck has a boat??
This is <u>not</u> Venice!!**

⬜⬜ "BABE? A B-O-A-T??"

"YES, BABE! You know? Them things that go on the water?"

⬜⬜ "Babe, I don't wanna go on a boat today."

"Why not, babe?? It'll be F-U-N?"

⬜⬜ "Babe, let's just go Number Eight tonight instead?"

"Yeah babe, we'll go there after. Come on. I'm in an Uber so I'll pick you up on the way."

Of course she fucking is.

⬜⬜ "Okay, fine. How long?"

"Half an hour… be ready.'

☐☐ "Kay, see you soon."

When pigs can fly.

"Bye babe!"

1:05pm.

It'll take AT LEAST an hour to get me out of these PJs…
forget the fucking make-up
and the hair circus.

I need a cigarette.

Where are my fucking cigarettes.

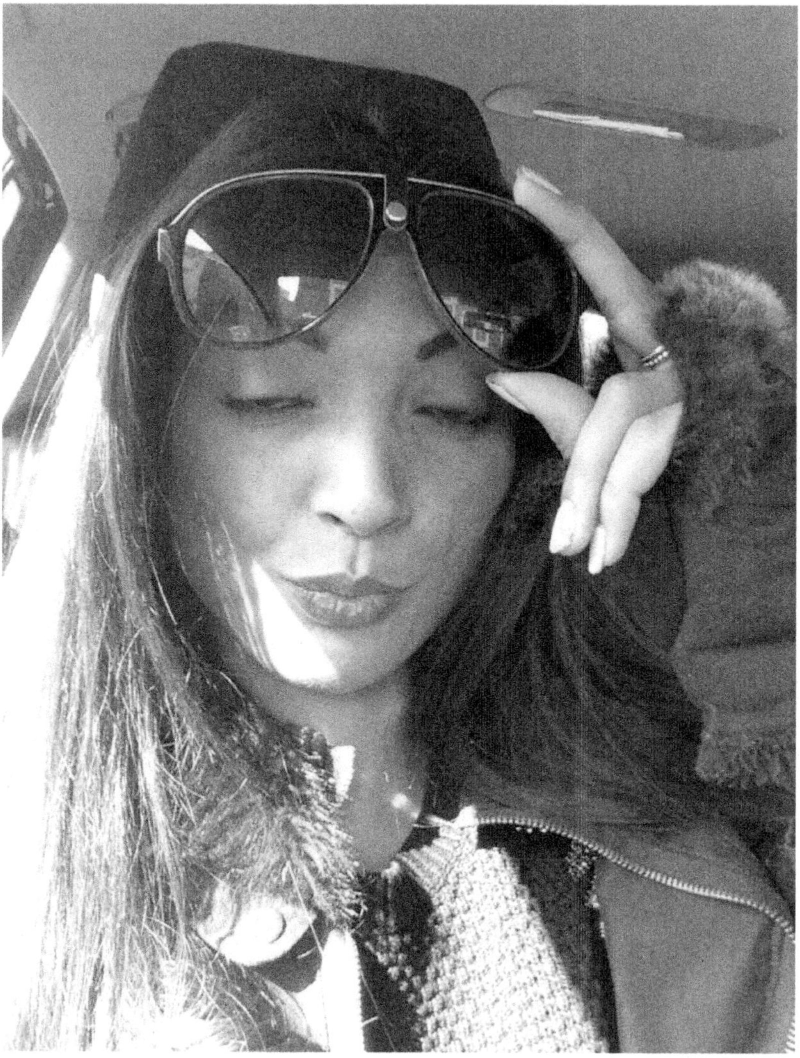

Waiting for the boat

This is not a boat.

It's a three-storey mansion with propellers.

"BABE, THAT'S NOT A B-O-A-T," I said.
"Yeah? It's a boat, babe?"
"Hey Zach!" Fi shouted.
A tall, dark gentleman emerged from the upper deck, sipping a glass of champagne.

He waved.

A second, much shorter and darker gentleman appeared behind him.

He also waved.

"That must be Bailey," Fi said.

"Fi.

Please tell me

it's not JUST THE FOUR OF US??"

"Yeah, babe. Why?"

OMFG.

It's a double date.

Imma kill her.

"Fi, I'm not going."
"Yeah you are… It'll be fun."

Sure.

If
'fun'
means
<u>being groped</u>
against my will
in the middle of the sea.

"Fi, you OWE me for this. I'm SERIOUS."
"BABE! RELAX! You're gonna have a great time."

Shoot me
in the fucking

head.

Sitting on the boat

Well, this is going well.

Note: If ever a sentence starts like that,
run for the hills.

I'm trying to apologise to 'Sir Captain Bailey' through his bedroom door.

He's locked himself inside.

He's holding the boat captive
until I apologise…

and mean it.

I couldn't care less,
except for the obvious.

I'm stuck on a boat, without Charlie.

"I'm sorry, Bailey.
I didn't mean it."

No answer.

This is ridiculous.

**This wouldn't
have happened
at Number Eight.**

"I was only joking, Bailey…"

Fucking Americans
and their
fucking
non-existent
sense of humour.

"I'm sorry."

You're a fucking idiot, Bailey.
I'm not sorry, Bailey.

But
I am

sorry

that you're behaving like

a three-year-old child.

The door swung open
to reveal a sour-faced Bailey.

"That's
C-A-P-T-A-I-N Bailey
to you!"
he said.

OMFG.

"Yes, SIR, CAPTAIN Bailey, Sir!" I said.

I gave him the
four finger salute.

"O-kay," he said.
"That's better."

"Now are you going to be a good little girl?" he said.

Go fuck yourself.

"Yes, SIR, CAPTAIN Bailey, Sir!" I said.

He eyed me suspiciously.
I smiled.
He swerved past me and went back to the crew.

Imma kill Fi.

Where the fuck is Charlie.

I spent the next few hours trying to think up ways to turn the boat around.

"Can't we just tell them there's an emergency at the restaurant?"
"No, babe. He knows where the restaurant is. He'll end up dropping us off."

This is desperate.

"FI! I CAN'T STAY ON THIS BOAT A MINUTE LONGER!!! I N-E-E-D to go home!!"
"Shhhh! They'll hear you."
"I don't care!

L-e-t them!"

Fi cupped her arm around my shoulder and pulled me in.
"Chill babe. Have another drink."
I looked around the ship.
Bailey's hiding out in the cockpit.
He's barely spoken more than two words since the incident.
Which means Zach has been attempting small talk about the intricacies of boat life maintenance
FOR THE PAST TWO HOURS.

I want to gauge my eyes out.

After a million lifetimes, I heard talk of mainland.

Finally.

It was getting dark and I just overheard Zach suggesting to Fi, 'if we're so tired' we could all go downstairs into the bedroom.

If we wanted to.

To the bedroom.

Three of us.

IF WE WANTED TO.

No fucking chance, mate.

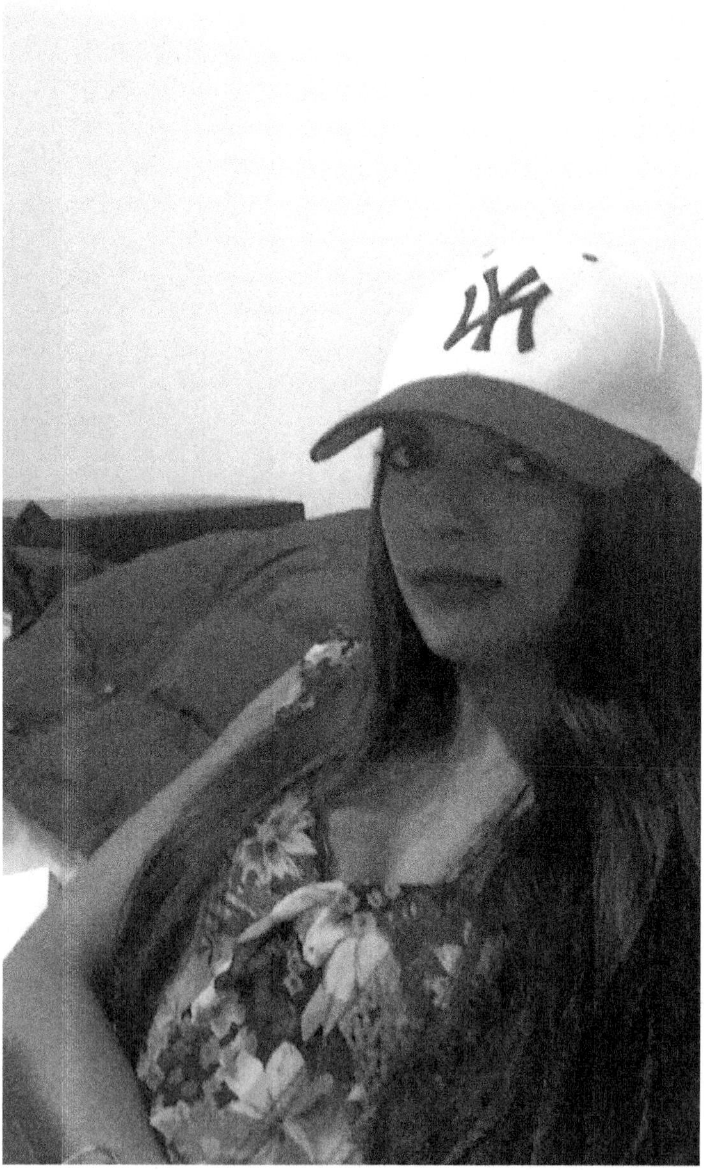

I put my feet up on the bench and stretched out.

There are actually stars here.

I never noticed that before.
I closed my eyes, but I was wide awake.
Full of champagne.
I'm not even remotely tired.

"Babe, you okay?" Fi asked.
"Yeah, I'm just tired."
I winked three times.
"Okay babe. What's up with your eye?"

FFS.

"NOTHING! I'm just…"

WINK WINK.

"Tired."

She stared blankly.
I got out my phone and sent her a message:

>**"I'm pretending I'm sleeping so they don't try anything."**

Fi looked at her phone.
She looked at me.

She smiled and nodded.

"O-K-A-Y babe," she said.
WINK, WINK.
"You should go to sleep."

"Thanks, honey. Wake me up when we get there, yeah?"

It was surprisingly hard to feign sleep. I ducked under a blanket and checked the phone light wasn't blaring through to the outside.

I don't have my earphones.
There's surprisingly little to do on here.

What do people DO
on here
ALL DAY??

Fi and Jono spent every waking minute swiping and tapping at their phones.
<u>They weren't answering my calls or liking any of my posts.</u>

What the fuck were they doing all this time?

Bored,
I sent out

the same message
to hundreds of people.

"Hey, how's you?"

I caught up on my unread mail.

I replied
to everyone
with the same message:

"Good. How's you?"

What now??

I have a message from Mr E??

How did I miss that??

"Hey Dheep.
It's your personal
wheelchair chauffeur service
here,
at your perusal.

(Inside joke)

When would you like to book your first test drive?"

Fuck yes.

"I'll be there in an hour."

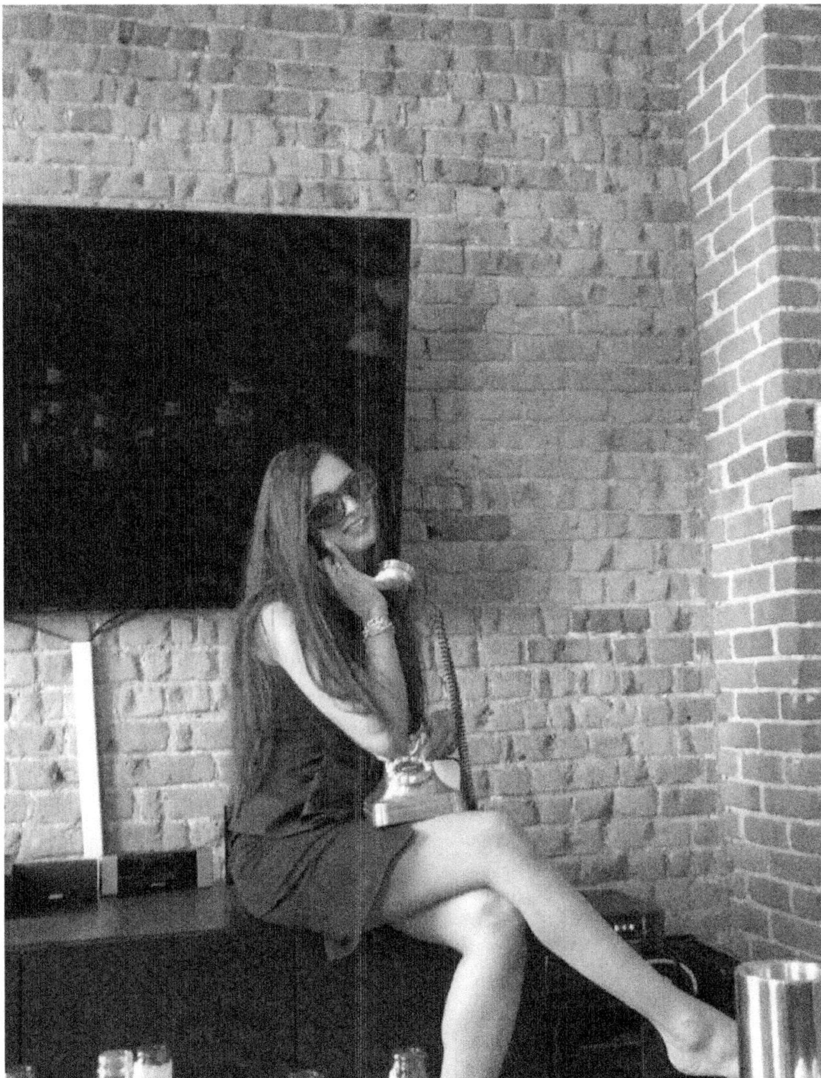

Standing at Mr E's door

Reality hits.

What the
fucking fuck
am I doing
standing
at Mr E's door
at 2am??

Ground.
Swallow.
Please.

Imma make a run for it.
Pretend it never happened.

You just
rang his bell,
moron…

and
announced yourself
to the
doorman.

Oh, fuck.

I'm fucking screwed then.

I reached into CC, to quickly check my face.

♡♡ Meet CC ♡♡

'CC' is the name of my Chanel purse.

CC is a living, breathing being.

CC is the most expensive friend I've bought, after Charlie.

Charlie out-expensed CC after about six months or so. I bought CC with my first New York bonus and she didn't even touch the sides.

You might overhear me using phrases like:

"CC's coming out tonight, fellas!"

"CC, that WHORE… she's got her flaps WIDE OPEN…"

"CC…

that THOT… She's ALWAYS ON HER BACK…"

CC has a tendency
of flinging herself across the floor
and pulling her flaps
wide open
until her
insides drip out.

CC is disgusting.

**She is certainly
one to watch.**

I'm at Mr E's apartment door

I hear the door chlocking.
I stuffed the compact back into CC and gently patted my nose.

WHOOOOSH.

The door opened, fanning my hair and floral dress. The skirt billowed around my waist to reveal my knickers....

OOPS.

I held my skirt against my thighs as I locked eyes with the silver-fox himself.

Hail Mary, full of GRACE.

HE IS FINE.

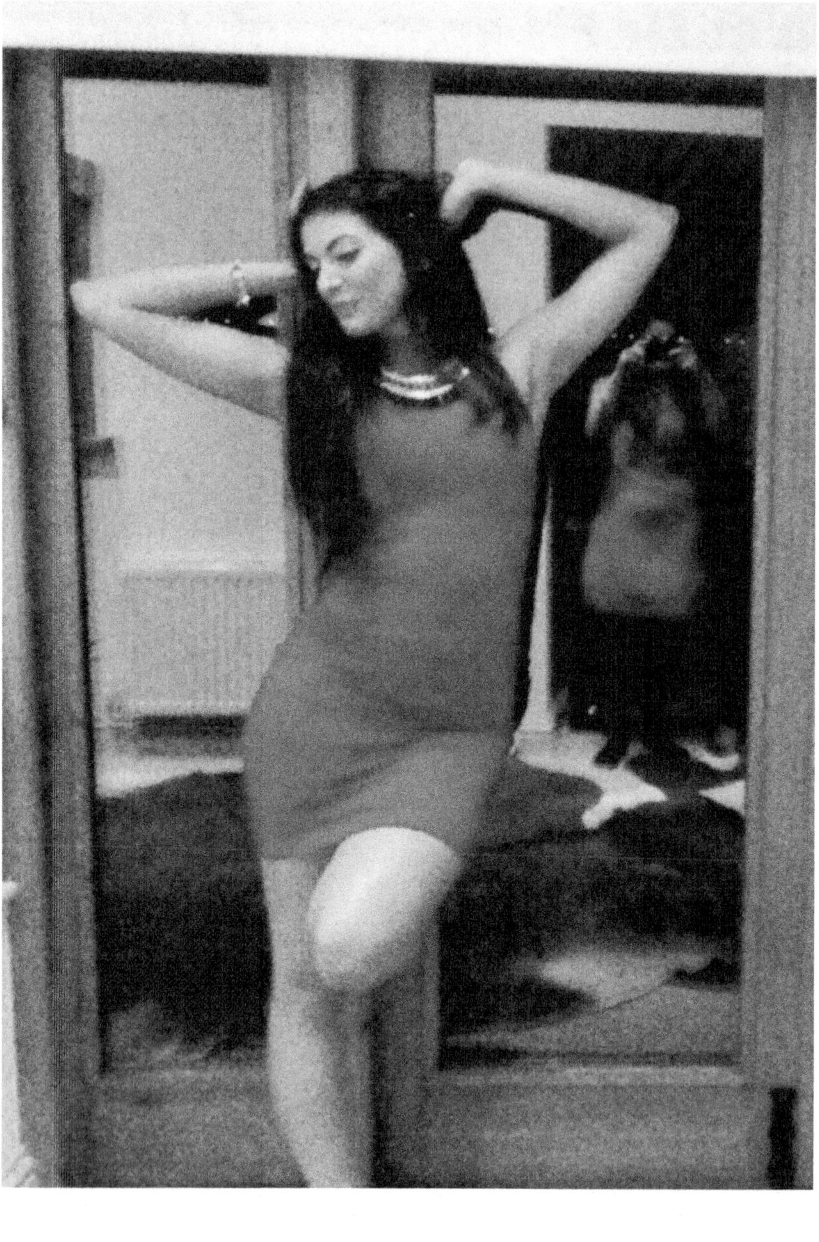

His eyes gripped my soul.

He smells like chocolate.

I love the way he's looking at me.

Like a vegan
tasting bacon
for the first time.

☐ **Meet Mr E** ☐

Mr E is a vision of black and gold, with flecks of white here and there.

Even his hair is gold.

I see it, peeking through his cap.
Like delicate strands of silk, glistening in the moonlight.

Bon Jovi '05 meets Patrick Bateman.
Perfect symmetry.

He's opted for a black and white Nirvana hoodie, which is flapping around his knees.
Distressed black denim and a slit at each knee.
Versace slippers.
Black, white and gold.
A backwards cap.
Drug dealer??

I hugged him.

He smells like chocolate.

I'm face to face with Mr E

"It's so nice to finally meet you,"
I said.

**It's so nice
to finally
meet you??**

I sound like my GRANDMA.

Moving swiftly on.

"I love what you've done with the place,"
I said.

**I love
what you've done
with the place??**

Fuck my life.

☐ Mr E's Apartment ☐

I'm sorry?

Am I
in Her Majesty's
Palace??

Or
New York
City??

Because… this <u>certainly</u> ain't Kansas no more…

Even his apartment is all gold.

There are more candlesticks than I can count.
As tall as me.
Dripping with hot pomegranate wax down their rustic sheaths.

Err…

<u>Midas called.</u>

He wants his shit back.

I spotted a tea set made of gold.

<u>Real gold.</u>

Not the fake kind.
The kind the Queen probably only saves for coronations…

It's
a fucking
literal
Gangster's paradise
in here.

It was sexual.

I'm in Mr E's apartment

I'm in Mr E's apartment.

I had to say that again.
Just to check it was real.

Two months have passed.

And we're finally meeting.

I've had friends get married with child in that time.
In fact, it's fairly common in NY.
Zero to bump plus ring in 30 days.
JJ for one.
Minus the bump…
so she says.

I sat on his couch.
It's wrapped in leopard's fur I think.

I wonder
how many animals
died
to make
his apartment
feel

this comfy.

I stretched out my legs across the sofa.
And leaned back.
I kicked off my heels.

**And
watched him
watching me.**

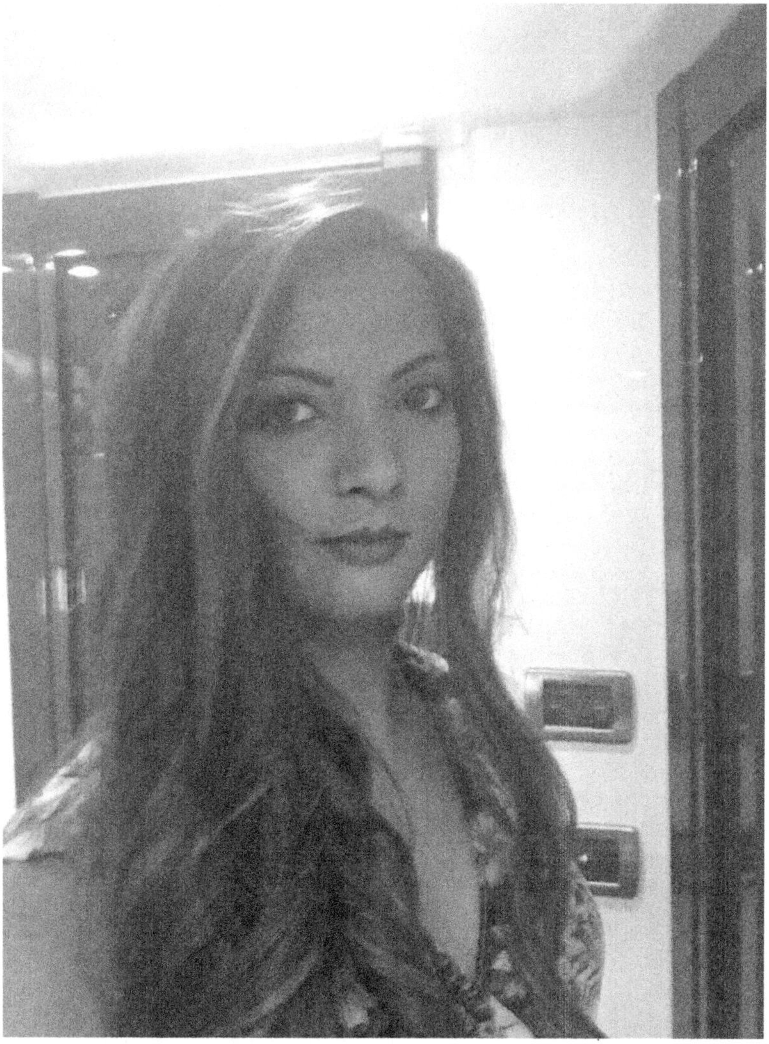

He's leaning over by the kitchen counter.

**Still
watching
me.**

"How's the champagne looking?"
I said.

He wiped his mouth with his fingertips and snapped into action.

"Of course, let me get that for you…

Dheep."

The <u>WAY</u> he said my name.

The next day in Mr E's apartment

I woke up on the same couch,

being smothered by a feline jungle.

Did I fall asleep?

I looked around the room for signs of life.
Charlie was still asleep on the coffee table, cuddling two straws.

Everything else was spotless.

All the glasses and dishes had been cleared away.

It was like it never happened.

I powdered my nose and scurried to the bathroom.
More cake required.
When I returned, Mr E was back leaning against the counter.

Watching me.

"Hey gorgeous,"
he said.

"H-e-y…"
I said,
covering as much of my face as possible, with my hair.

How do I get out of here.

I'll just wait for him to 'ask me what I'm doing today'. AKA 'My cue to leave'.

Part of me wants to stay.

All of me wants to stay.

I'm also just a little concerned that I…

really do love him.

"I was just taking this little guy for a walk," he said.

Gucci galloped towards me, jingling all the way, stood up on his hind legs and started pawing at my knees.

☐ **Meet Gucci** ☐

Gucci is what happens when a Gremlin and a bunny rabbit mate.

He's
a snotty
little monster.

He's also the most adorable little fucker you've ever seen.

And he'll make you laugh something chronic.

Once you get past the constant drooling, farting and snoring,

you're looking at
the Daffy Duck
of the canine club.

French bulldogs.

Everyone in the city has one.
It's the new black.

People overlook the fact they're test-tube babies.
It doesn't matter that they're genetically engineered to look this cute…

because they are

so
cute…

If only they could genetically engineer them not to fart so much.

Back to Mr E's apartment

I scooped Gucci up into my arms and took him to the couch for a cuddle.

Little Fartface.

I tried to think up places I needed to be…

Just delete his number…
forget him…
walk away…

just walk away

now
before
it's too late…

"You hungry?"
he said.

Too late.

"Umm…m-a-y-b-e-…"
I said.

Far too late.

"Cool,"
he said.

"There's a nice brunch spot,"
he said.

"Would you like to go with me,"
he said.

"Unless you have other plans today?"

**Of course I fucking don't have
any
other
plans.**

Unless

**watching
romcoms
and
crying**

<u>into</u>
<u>my</u>
<u>Cheetos</u>

counts as **'having plans'**.

> "Um… I could go with you,"
> I said.

> "Cool,"
> he said.

He's turning around to face the sink.
He's been faffing around there for quite some time.
What is he doing??

He's
washing
the dishes,
for crying out
loud.

Foam

**is frothing up
his forearms,
for Christ's
sake.**

I fanned myself with my hands.

He turned his head to say something.

"I just need to run the
hoover round
real quick
and then we can go."

FML.

At Tao with Fi

I haven't heard from Mr E.
It's been 5 days.

Five days.

We're supposed to be on a date tonight.
But he never text.

Arsehole.

So now I'm out with Fi

and I can't get him out of my head.

I've tried to delete his number

five times.

I have not been successful…
yet.

"Are you **sure** you're supposed to meet tonight?"

Fi asked.

I'm not a fucking MORON, Fi.

"Well, y-e-ah, that's what he said last Sunday."

I can't believe this is happening.

I'd swirled the lychee around until it looked like slushed up remains of someone's large intestine.

"Did you ASK him about it?"
she said.

"No!"
I said, annoyed.
"Why should I have to ask him??
If he wants to see me,
then he'll make the effort to see me."

"Just ask him, babe."

I'm not fucking asking him anything.

"No, I can't...
He's CLEARLY just not interested."
I said.

I dragged Fi to the bathrooms.
I ushered her into my cubicle, careful the attendant wasn't looking.
She's preparing lines over on the shelf by the toilet paper dispenser.

I have to wonder

**what else
is that
empty shelf
used for??**

"Do you think I should just message him then?"
I asked her.

Fi handed me the straw.

"Yes, hunny.
Just ask him when you're meeting…
or just go over there."

Yeah.
What's the harm in
one
**tiny
message…**

"NO FI!
Haven't you seen that movie,
'I'm Just Not That into You'?"
I said.

"Nah, I haven't seen it, babe."

"Well, watch it and then talk to me.
I'm NOT going to contact him."

I'm not going to chase him.

I should delete his number now, just in case…

"Babe,
just ask him
what he's doing tonight?"
she said,
beckoning me to leave.

We washed our hands and tipped the attendant.
Then we hung back at the bathroom bar.

Tao, Downtown, has a bar in the bathrooms which separates the entrance to the male and female bathrooms.

It's usually a great place

to get better acquainted with someone you met over by the public bar.

Not so ideal, I found, if **their girlfriend** ALSO decides to use the bathrooms shortly after.

That was slightly awkward for all involved.

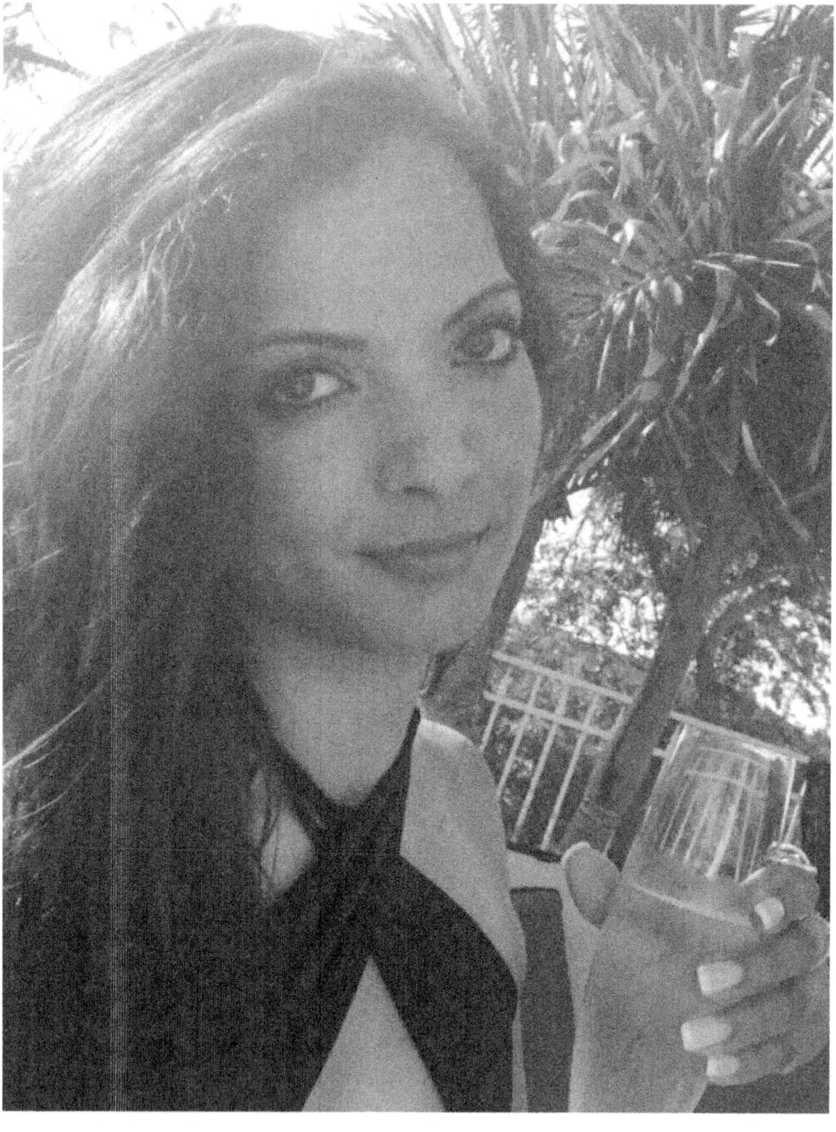

"It's dead in here,"
Fi said.

I shrugged my eyebrows and continued to annihilate the lychee.

"Did you ask him?
Your guy?"
she said.

I gave her a look.

"At least we can go chill there?"
she said.

"We can chill at mine,"
I said abruptly,
picking the last slither
of lychee out of the glass
with the pick.

"Tell him to bring some friends
to come chill too,"
she said.

"Fi?
Really??
Come on,"
I said.

I dismissed her comment and put the glass down.
I looked around at the crowd that had culminated behind us.

All paired up already.

"Alright, fine,"
I said.

He replied an hour later.

It's on.

Pleading with the doorman

I knew this was a bad idea.

"Ma'am, he's not answering his phone.

Are you sure you're supposed to be meeting him tonight?"

The doorman said.

"Yes, I'm sure!"

I flashed him the text message from Mr E on my phone. "Check the time - it was sent just an hour ago."

This is so fucking embarrassing.

JUST ANSWER YOUR BUZZER ALREADY!!

The doorman glanced at the screen and then looked again at me.

"That could be

from anyone."

WHAT THE ACTUAL FUCK.

I should never have let Fi talk me into this.

"I'm sorry ma'am," he said, his eyes shoo-ing me away.

"You can try calling his phone," he said, looking at the person in line behind me.

"If you have his number."

Fucking kill me now, you dick.

"Sir," I said, smiling sweetly and reaching my hand over the desk, "couldn't you just let us up this once, please?"

He looked at my hand in contempt.

"No miss. I cannot.

These are the rules.

Now if you could please step aside, there are other guests waiting."

He quickly dismissed me and served the other guests.

I FUCKING HATE YOU ETHAN.

I gruffly picked up my phone from the counter and walked towards the exit, gesturing Fi to follow.

I've already called him three times.

I'm NOT calling again.

I sent him a text.

"Ethan, we're leaving.
We waited here for twenty minutes. Goodbye."

I'm deleting his number RIGHT NOW.

And I'm NEVER

SPEAKING TO HIM AGAIN.

Chapter Three: Dating

Two days later, Fourth of July weekend

What time is it?
I reached for my phone.

"Morning, babe! What do you wanna do today, hunny?" Fi said.

Fi's still here.

Why is Fi still here??

She's working away on her phone, strewn across the sofa.

Why is Fi up at this ungodly hour??

The sun is up.

Why is the sun still up??

I should be going to bed…
"What time is it?" I said,
"Eleven thirty, babe."

It's practically dawn.

The place is a mess.
Takeout and cigarettes everywhere.

"I need a smoke."

I rolled over off the bed and perched myself on the windowsill.
I looked out at my bench outside Joe's coffee shop.
Two fellas juggling balls.

I love that bench.

☐ Meet My Apartment ☐

About my housing situation...

I basically live in a box.

Not a very big box either.
At least it's bigger than my last box.
My ex called my last box a prison cell...
He wasn't far off... I would have preferred a prison cell though.

At least you see friends in prison.

My previous box was no larger than 150 square feet.

150 square feet.

There are
FOOD TRUCKS
bigger than that.

The interior decor was strictly 1800s, complete with an army of creepy crawlies.

The crawlies were **an added feature.**

Spiders I can handle. But cockroaches?

Fuck no.

"Are you SURE there aren't any cockroaches?" I asked my broker.

He promised me.

"Because if I find any… I have your number." I said.

He laughed.

It isn't funny.

"I

<u>will</u>
call you
if I
find
ANY."

   I looked at him apprehensively before I signed on the dotted line.
   The next morning after I moved in…

<u>NO FUCKING JOKE, I SWEAR.</u>

Mr Roach Himself.

2am.

On the kitchen floor.

<u>I'M FUCKING LIVID.</u>

He's taking a breather on my kitchen floor…

It took me about TWO HOURS to pluck up the courage to stand up to him.

I chased him with a broom.

He told me to fuck off and hid in my closet with all my clothes.

Brilliant.

I spent
the whole night
wondering
when
he was going to
fly
into my mouth.

Those fuckers can fly.

Someone at work told me.

The next morning, he was right back where he started.

In the kitchen, having a breather, in the exact same spot.

When the delivery man arrived to install my new bed, I cornered him before I let him inside.

"You gotta help me," I said.
"Th-theres a … cockroach," I said.

He went running the other way.

"NAH MAN, I don't DO cockroaches, I'm outta here!" he said.

No fucking kidding.

He ended up putting on a brave face and, before I could stop him, he stomped on Mr Roach.
Sending his entrails flying across my brand-new apartment.
Which meant, for the next year I was forever discovering its babies, all round the apartment.

Nice.

My favourite was their morning bath time.

Every morning, twenty something baby roaches flying around the bath like they owned the fucking place.

Don't even get me started on Harry.

<u>Harry was my resident MOUSE.</u>

I choked on my salad the day the day we met.

He ran across my feet during dinner.

Eating takeout on my bed,

with Netflix perched on a garden chair.

He made a run for my closet…
apparently everyone's favourite place.

And then taking a bath on my kitchen floor.

Mr Roach is laughing in his grave.

I tried to break my lease.

My broker said
I'd have better luck
getting a divorce.

"I'm not married," I told him.

"Exactly."

That's what $2500 a month buys in New York City.

A fucking box of

cockroaches.

Thankfully I met Charlie.
So, falling asleep wasn't a problem anymore.

**Neither was
waking up
with a mouthful of roaches
and a rodent's nest in my panties.**

As soon as my lease was up, I moved 100 footsteps away to the next block.
Paid an extra $1,000 a month and said goodbye to the roaches.

Three floors off the ground,
100 extra square feet

and peace of fucking mind.

Upgraded to the 21st century interior decor, complete with a doorman, an on-site gym, on-site laundry and a private rooftop terrace.

●●○○○ T-Mobile LTE
17:00
57%
udr.com
ROOFTOP TERRACE
Next Gallery
6 of 6

T-Mobile LTE
16:59
57%
udr.com
ROOFTOP TERRACE
Previous Gallery
1 of 6

Yes
I know,
I'm
an
actual
G.

The setup was pretty cool too.
I liked to get decor inspiration from the sexy man across the street.

His apartment was right opposite mine,
so, we liked to cook dinner at the same time,
avoiding eye contact as much as possible.

I think he kept his curtains open

just so I could
watch him
undress.

So, I did the same.

Just kidding.

But that could have been fun.

I especially loved how every morning at 6am he would carefully place each of his twenty-something pillows and cushions across half of the bed.
And then every night took them down, one by one, and lay them to rest on the couch.
He also had a white, silk curtain divider between the bed and the couch which I hadn't yet got around to finding.
But I loved the idea.

Apartment goals.

This is my new apartment.

Except I switched up the layout quite a bit.

That, in the top left is my kitchen area.
I never got around to buying any breakfast bar stools either.
The bottom left is my new bathroom.
No roaches in there.
To the right of that is my new closet.

My closet is practically the same size as my last apartment.

The above lounge/bedroom layout made
zero sense.

What's the point in having a TV when you can't watch it comfortably??

So, I stuck it where the couch is and instead put the couch at the foot of the bed, so it was now facing the TV.

I also got a Queen bed and moved it to the centre of the cubby it's in.

I love my new place.

And I don't have to share it.

Back to my apartment

"Babe, let's go brunch?" Fi said.
"Where?" I said.
"Your roof."
"Yeah?"
"We'll get some food, get some wine, get some music and go sit up on the roof and tan… it's such a nice day, babe!"

Fuck it.

"Yeah, I'm cool with that." I said.
Anything to stop me thinking of Mr E…

The words:

"I'm really sorry,"

flashed across my phone screen.

Unknown number.

It has to be Mr E.

I slammed the phone down without reading it.

"Was it Mr E, babe?" Fi said.

I didn't say anything.

"Babe?" she asked again.

My eyes nodded for me.
"What did he say?"

"I dunno."

It's been 2 days.

Zero fucks given.

Fi picked up my phone.
Why did I give her my passcode.

"Fi, just leave it… I'm done with it."

"He says he's sorry…" Fi said.

"Babe…he seems really sorry," Fi said again, looking up.

She flashed the screen to JJ.

"I don't care. I'm still done," I said.

I folded my arms across my chest and looked away.

"Babe… come on… he seems r-e-a-l-l-y nice…" Fi said.

WTF?!?
WHO'S SIDE ARE YOU ON??

"You don't even know him!"

She shrugged and handed me back my phone.

Oh.
I See.

He's invited 'all of my girlfriends' over

for free booze
and free food.

To watch the fireworks.

To apologise.

"We're not going," I said.
Fi and JJ shrieked in unison.

"You don't A-C-T-U-A-L-L-Y BELIEVE HIM, do you??"

I said.

"YES babe," Fi said,
"If he says he fell asleep, then he fell asleep…"

Oh, fucking wake up and smell the HORSESHIT, FI!

"I know these music guys…"
she said.
"They work all day and all night on their beats for days on end and then they get so tired they fall asleep …
it happens."

The sun has fried her brain.

"What else are we gonna do?" she said.

"Yeah, we can't see the fireworks from here anyway. We may as well just go there?" JJ chimed in.

"Okay, F-I-N-E."

The girls cheered and danced around the terrace with their drinks.

"But don't BLAME ME<u> </u>when he 'falls asleep'

<u>again</u><u> </u>

and we're left out

on the street….

<u>again</u>."

Arriving at Mr E's apartment

I didn't even say 'hi'.
I waltzed passed him, picked up one of his caps and looked in the floor-to-ceiling mirror.
I put it on my head.

Sexy.

I stretched across the sofa.

Shoes off.
Feet up.
Sat back.

And
what.

He's leaning against the kitchen counter, peeking at me from beneath the tip of his cap.

Take a good look.
Ethan.

He won't look me in the eyes.

Good.

Go fetch me a drink, boy.

"What would you girls like to drink?" he asked, suddenly standing to attention.

"Champagne," I said.

His tats are out.
A python slithering in a bed of roses.
Curling its girth around a withered skull.
Full sleeve.

He returned with a gold tray, encrusted with crystals.
Filled with different liquors.

He took out a bottle of champagne.

He held the cork between his fingers, gently teasing the barrel in his free hand.

Good with his hands.

He wet the glass.
To give me a taste.

As he poured,
tremors,
through me.

When he finished,
he wrapped it in a napkin,
embroidered with his initials,
and tucked it away
into its home.

A dry ice bucket,
Made from black crystal.

I raised my glass to his.

He
watched me
drink

from his glass.

The sushi came.

The entire coffee table was laced with trays and trays, tiers and tiers of sushi bites.
Each one crystal, with a golden rim.

It's the Noah's Ark of the sushi world.

Who knew Versace made dishes…
and cutlery…

Each tray was a masterpiece,
a work of art.

Fucking Versace.

And that's how Mr E, got his
new name.

Versace.

After dinner mints

Charlie also made it to dinner.
Dinner's not dinner without Charlie.

But tonight, I had to decline.

"I have work tomorrow," I said.

A good little girl.

I can be responsible and well behaved, sometimes.

Why am I

always

the only one who has to work??

I need to make new friends…

Fi and JJ went out to the balcony for a cigarette break.

Great.
A few minutes **alone** with Versace.

I strolled around the room with my champagne glass.
Stroking his ornaments.

Why does he have a picture of a cow??

Hung on the wall behind him was a painting of a cow, grazing in a field. It was encased with a luscious, thick, gold frame.

Next to it was a huge brass shield, as tall as my torso. It was ornate with a golden coat of arms. And pierced through its heart were two swords in the shape of an 'x'.

"Is that your family's coat of arms?" I asked him.

I hadn't noticed I was fingering the bottom of my dress, crinkling it against my nails.

With one quick movement,

he hooked his hand around my waist, gripped my dress with his fist and swept me over his lap.

I landed in his arms.
I rested my head in his neck.

He smells like chocolate.

I curled my legs over one of the armrests and cuffed one foot over the other.

I softly stroked my right hand across his jaw, watching as his stubble prickled against my fingertips.

I pressed my head deeper into his neck and kissed his nook.

I feel his hand on cheek as he strokes my hair.

Gentle.

I looked up at his lips.

I want him to kiss me so much.

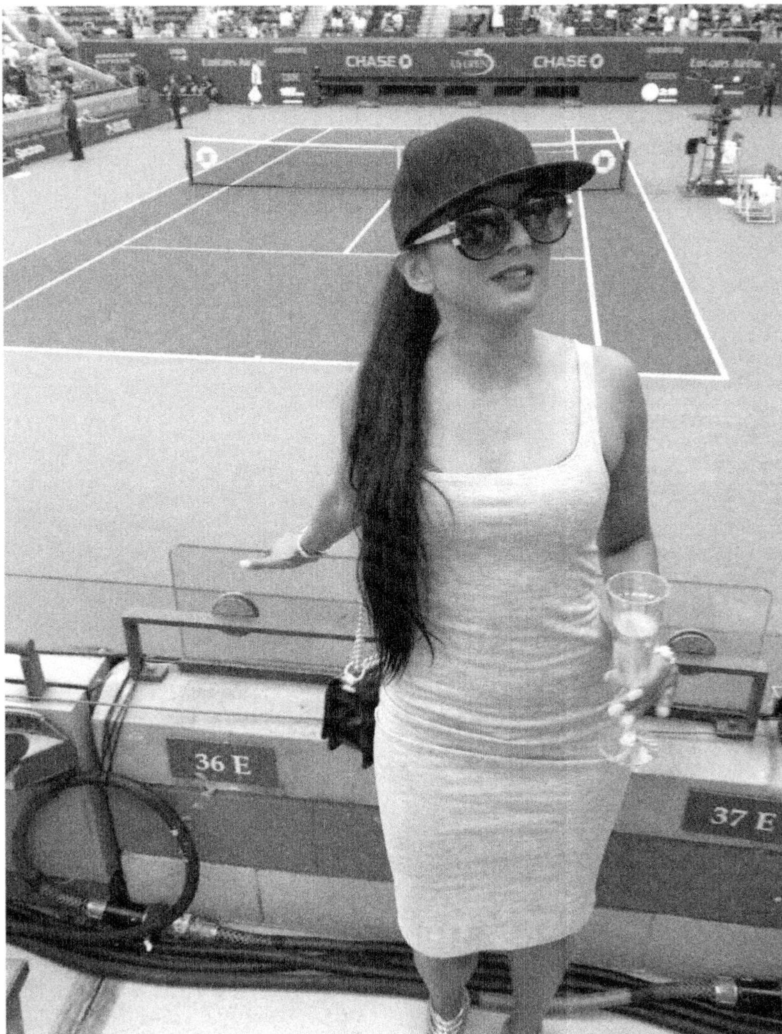
CHASE
CHASE
36 E
37 E

I straightened myself up to look at him.
His eyes are examining my face.
I see them circling past my eyes, my nose, my cheek, my lips.
He stroked my neck with the back of his hand and his eyes soon followed it as it moved and rested on the top of my dress.

I heard the door open, followed by a wave of hot air.

"Woah, it's HOT out there!"

JJ !*#?!

My head fits so perfectly.
I closed my eyes
and listened,
to his heart beat.

His fingers are circling around my knee,
around my thigh,
and back again.

I'm
home.

We're outside, saying goodbye.

The girls are waiting in the car and we're stood a metre outside the entrance,
saying nothing.

"Thank you for coming," he said.

I continued to play with my curl.

"Sure" I said.

"Just don't fuck it up next time."

There's a knot in my hair.
Shit.

He stopped me by pushing the curls behind my neck.
His fingers paused on my neck.

> "Thank you
> for giving me
> another chance…
> you didn't have to,"
> he said.

He moved in and kissed my cheek.

I caught his hand between mine and kissed his fingertips.

"Goodnight," he said.

"Goodnight."

He walked me to the car and helped me inside. He closed the door and waved us goodbye.

Getting my nails did

"Jungle Red!"
I squealed,
as I presented my talons.

Ivy (pronounced like ee-v-ee) is the most talented nail technician in New York City.
She was also my first friend in New York City.

She doesn't know that.

I've been seeing her for over a year now, nearly every week.

"Girl,
we don't do that shade here…"
she said, rolling her eyes and tapping away at her phone.

"I know.. It's a - never mind."

I let all my troubles float away.

"Soo…" I said.

"I met a
guy!"

I squealed.

Ivy paused briefly, with the emery board in her hand, and looked up at me.

"SHUT THE FRONT DO-OR!"

She said, in her thick Brooklyn accent.

"Well tell me everything!" she added.

"Well his name is Ethan… I forget his last name…"

Do I even know his last name??

I tried to remember his occupation.

"Something to do with houses… managing them, I think…"

"But he's a music producer too…"

What does he DO again??

"Is he single?"
she asked, looking at me accusingly.

"Of course!
I mean…
I didn't specifically ask…
but I'm assuming…"

"Mmm hmm,"
she said.

She resumed her filing.

The store manager, Sarah, appeared and came to sit with us.

"What did I miss?" Sarah said.

"I met a guy!" I said, squealing and bopping in the seat.

"Oh, yahh?" she said.

She snapped her gum and picked up an emery board. She started filing her nails.

"And is he single?"

she asked.

What the fuck.

"She doesn't know," Ivy said, giving her side eye.

Seriously, what the fuck.

"Uh, well… I'm guessing he has to be or we wouldn't be seeing each other, no?" I said.

Sarah stopped filing and reached over, gently cupping her hand over one of mine.

"Next time you're there, you check his mail, check his trash, Anything. Anything you can find. The smallest

hint
of a female presence. Mmmkay?"

Sarah said.

She removed her hand and sat back into her stool. She and Ivy silently nodded to one another.

"Oh…kay," I said meekly.

"Like, what is his furniture like?" Sarah asked.

"It's really lush, it's like a palace,"

"Let me stop you there, girl-friend," Sarah said, waving her emery board in the air.

"Right," I said.

"I was dating this guy once, I met him on this dating site, Coffee Meets Cake and …"

<u>Sarah launched into a 30-minute story about her ex-boyfriend.</u>

"And, anyway… he gave me this ring and everything cos we'd been dating a whole year now…

but it turns out
he had a wife
and kids
in this whole other city
I didn't even know about.

I just thought he liked to travel a lot…
you know,
with work?

Boy, did I feel stupid…
So, you gotta be REAL careful you know, girl…
Now I make sure I DO MY HOMEWORK…"

"Yah, girl," Ivy said, chiming in.

Ivy added,

"You know I was dating this guy for a whole year…

A WHOLE YEAR,

before I found out
he was a
hitman."

There are no words.

"Was he married too?" I asked her.

"Nah girl… but I nearly married him."

"There you go, all finished," Ivy said.

Getting ready for our date

My phone started ringing.
Ouch.
I put the curlers down and ran my finger under the cold tap as I haphazardly answered the phone with my other hand.

Facetime:
Versace

FACETIME??
OH SHIT!

"Hi there gorgeous!" he said.
Versace's head and shoulders flooded my screen.

The way he smiles at me.

I spotted my thumbnail.

Oh, shit,
I'm a monster!

I hunt for better lighting.

"Hey you… I was just in the middle of doing my hair…" I said, covering my hand with my face as I moved.

"Are you looking forward to our dinner tonight?" he asked.

"Ummm… yes?" I said.

Who FaceTimes without an appointment??

"Good. Me too…I just wanted to see your face." He said.

I smiled and tried to find a better angle.

Jono rolled his eyes.

He was sat on the sofa, drinking wine out of my red mug.
I tried to hush him.
He stuck his fingers in his mouth and pretended to vom.

"Okay, bye gorgeous," Versace said.

"Bye!"

"Don't be late!" he added, before waving and hanging up.

"You guys make me wanna vom,"
Jono said,

taking another gulp.

◻◻ Meet Jono ◻◻

Jono is gender fluid.

He used to just be gay, but I think that means something else now.

I'm not allowed to call him gay either.

Which is fine.

But now every guy I date wants to know why Jono is allowed to watch me shower

but they are not.

Just to clarify,

JONO DOES NOT WATCH ME SHOWER.

<u>I can't emphasise that enough.</u>

Nor can I tell you exactly how many times that very sentence has left my mouth.

JONO DOES NOT WATCH ME SHOWER.

I'll say that again,
just in case it didn't get through...

JONO DOES NOT WATCH ME SHOWER.

Because I know you're going to ask me a hundred more times before I break it off with you.

Jono is usually around when I shower.

I'm not gonna lie.

BUT
JONO DOES NOT WATCH ME SHOWER.

That's one of the perks isn't it?
Of having a male friend that is repulsed at the sight of you naked?
You can walk around, as free as a bird.

Naked as the day you were born.

Which I must point out,

HAS NEVER HAPPENED.

It's different from having a female friend because <u>he's not secretly jumping for joy every time you look shit without make-up on.</u>

And he definitely isn't taking a picture,
just to surprise you with later when he's having a bad day
and just generally feels like **<u>being a dick</u>**.

And he's definitely not archiving it in his memory and bringing it up in conversation whenever anyone ever has something nice to say about you.

"Yeah, I guess she looks nice…
but you should see her without make-up…
<u>she looks nothing like that IRL…</u>"

That's why he's my best friend.

He doesn't approve of any guy who tries to date me.
He loves everything fashion.
He loves anything J-Pop.

*** Don't ask me what that is ***

He's LITERALLY the ONLY person I will ever take shopping…
EVER.
He holds all my bags and waits for endless hours while I try out the entire store…
which is everything **he** has picked out for me …
and then gives me the full
'thumbs up, thumbs down' service.

He's my best friend in the world.

He's always blowing everyone else off to come and hang with me, because we have way more fun.

My door is always open,
the wine is always chilling
and Charlie is always available.

He's my brother from another mother.

Getting me ready for my date

I lifted my mug to his.
We clinked them together.

"Chin chin,"

we said together, before taking a sip.

"So **who** are you doing tonight?" I asked.

Jono continued swiping through his phone.
I snapped my fingers in front of his phone.

"JONO?"

"Yeah yeah, girl. Keep your panties on," he said.

He tapped what appeared to be a quick message and then put the phone down on his lap.

"SO.
Tonight.
I'm supposed to be meeting this Russian guy
from Grindr at 8
and then I'm hanging
with Luav around 9."

He flashed me the screen, which revealed a topless young man covering his face with a book.

"Nice," I said.

"How's it going with Lavo?" I asked.

Who the fuck is Lavo?

"LUAV," he said sternly.

Which one is he again??

"Sorry, Luav… Going well?"

"Yeah, good. This'll be our…" he paused for a few seconds, "third date now."

"WOW. Third date? Sounds serious, for you?"

"Yeah…. Actually, you're right. I didn't think of it that way…"

Silence.

"But it's just casual, you know? This is New York City, after all."

The sound of wine pouring.

"So, is this your first official date with Versace?"

"Yeah I guess so," I said, mid-curl.

I touched up my lippie and jujjed my hair in the mirror.

Outfit number two?

"I guess the first two don't really count as dates as there were other people around?" I called out as I changed outfits.

"Yeah, totally," he said.

"What do you think of this one?" I asked him.

He shook his head and waved his finger, gesturing me back into the closet.

**Damn.
I love that dress.**

"Did you find out if he's seeing anyone else?" Jono shouted from the sofa.

Fucking, seriously??

"No!!" I yelled.

I pulled the second dress over my head.

"Do you think I should ask him?"

Silence.

"JONO??"

"Sorry, I was just texting.
No, you don't need to, but **he probably is seeing other people.**"

"WHAT?? Why would you say that??"

"This is New York City honey. Everybody is seeing someone else."

Not me.

I slurped my wine.

"What about this one?" I asked.

"It's fine."

FFS.

"FINE??"
I said.

"Don't you have that sexy green dress? That lacey Ted Baker one with the big zip down the front...?" he said, gesturing me away.

I looked at my watch.
Shit, no time.

"I was supposed to be there ten minutes ago. FUCK," I said.

Supermarket sweep.
I sped into the bathroom, scooping as much make-up as I could inside CC.
My favourite powder smashed all over the floor.
Crap.
I scooped up the still-in-tact, larger chunks of powder and shoved them back into the compact, then threw it in the bag.
I switched off the curlers and grabbed my fags, keys and phone.
Two messages from Versace.
Double crap.

"Come on, Jono. We have to go!"

I downed the rest of my mug and balanced it out with a line of Charlie.

"JONO, COME... ON...!"

He downed his drink and started collecting his things.

"Yeah, yeah.

**This girl
is moving
as fast as she can,"**
he said.

Chapter Four: Falling

Our first date

When my Uber pulled up, he opened the door.
His hand reached out for me, before I was even ready to leave.

Red carpet treatment.

His
hand
was firm,

he steadied me
with his grip.

He pulled me up and into his arms.
He kissed both cheeks and whispered in my hair,

"You're gorgeous," he said.

"Thank you,"
I said, gushing.
"So are you."

He kept his hand on the small of my back as he gently ushered me to the door.
The host blocked the doorway.
He darted towards Versace and sharply shook his hand.

"Hey man!" He said.

He slapped Versace on the shoulder with his other hand.

"Hey Med! How's it going, man??" Versace said.

"Good good! What happened to you, bro? You used to be in here every day?" Med said.

Versace smiled at me and then looked back at Med.

"I know, man… been busy with this beautiful woman."

He pulled me under his arm and squeezed my shoulder.

He introduced me and added, "Med owns the restaurant."

"Hi Med, lovely to meet you," I said, shaking his hand and smiling sweetly.

"Lovely to meet you, Dheep. Come this way…
We have your usual table for you, Ethan,"
Med said, gesturing us inside.

The table had room for at least six more people.
It was a long table at the very front of the restaurant, looking right out onto the street.
There were two long benches running the full length of the table and one small bench on one of the shorter sides by the wall. Each bench was lined with silk cushions, coloured in magenta, fuchsia and burnt orange, with gold detailing.
It had a shisha bar sort of feel.
This is my kind of place.
It felt cosy and warm.

Intimate.

"Shall we?" Versace said, gesturing for me to climb in.

He pulled the bench out as far as it would go and steadied me from behind, with one hand supporting my back and the other for me to lean on. Then he skooched in to the small bench on the end, at a right angle to me.

**Every breath
he spoke
was like
<u>Charlie</u>
to me.**

I can't remember anything he said.

**But it was beautiful,
every word.**

We took thousands of selfies.

I found them the next day.
We weren't legible in any of them, not one.
But you could just about make out our teeth, laughing.
Or grinning.

It was cute.

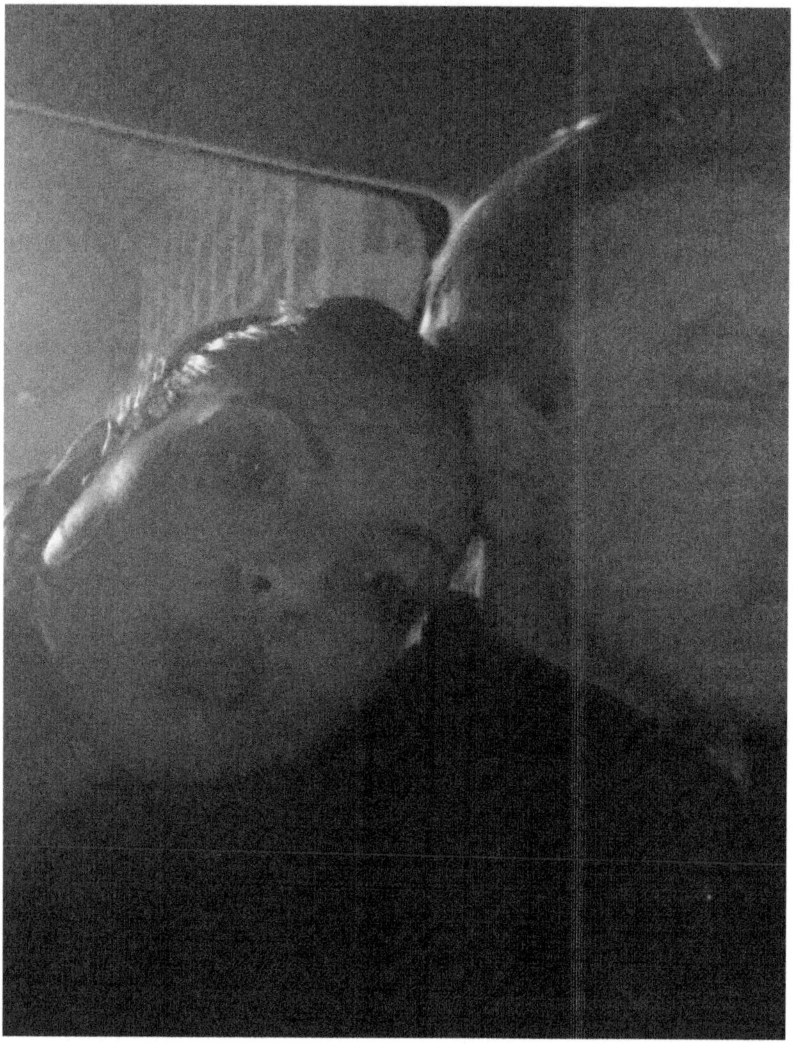

At Versace's Apartment

He likes Chocolate.
I like Charlie.

It should never work.

Hours and hours passed like that.

Charlie and Chocolate.
Charlie and Chocolate.
Charlie and Chocolate.
Charlie and Chocolate.

We talked until the moon finally gave way to the sun.

We're talking shit again.

I just discovered Versace used to be in a Spanish boy band.

"Yeah! It's ridiculous, right? I couldn't even speak Spanish!" he said.
"And then we."

"OH MY GOSH

can we listen to it?

Is it on
YouTube?"

I pulled out my phone and started typing Versace's full name into YouTube.

"Yeah so then we actually," he said.

"What was the band called again?

Imma
find it
now,
I SWEAR!"

I said.

**I JUST FUCKING LOVE THIS DAY
SO MUCH!!!!**

**WHAT A FUCKING DAY
TO BE ALIVE!!!**

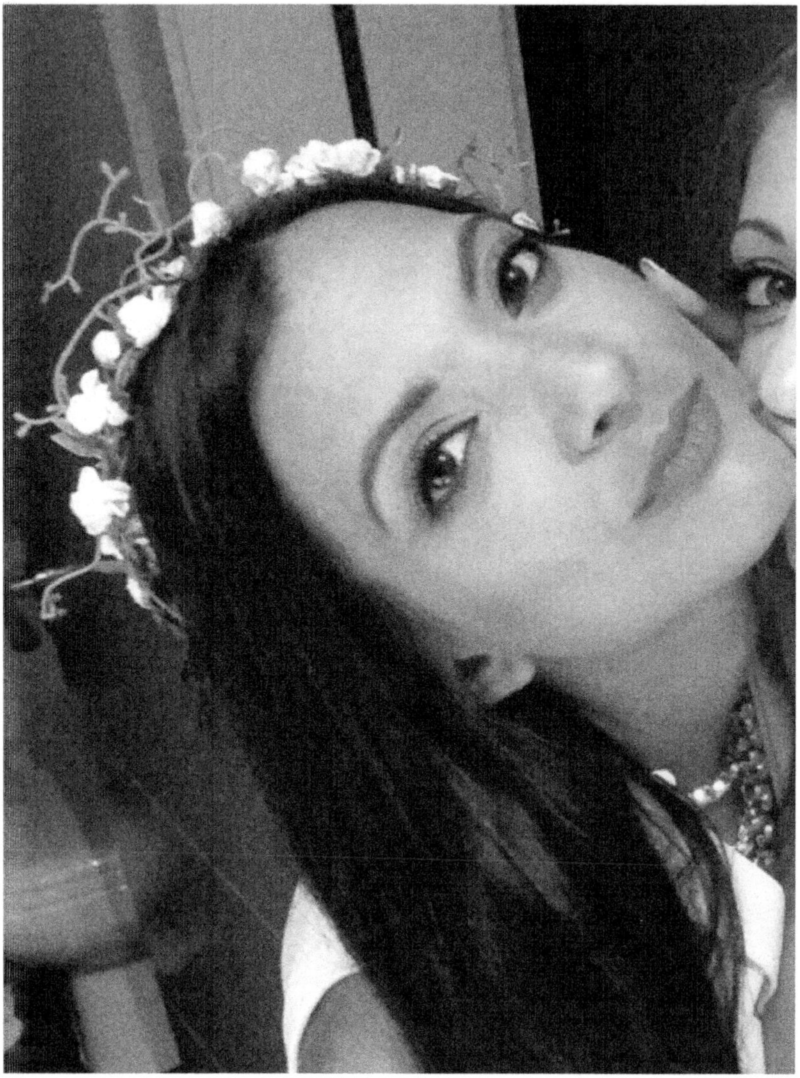

He coughed.

"And then we -" he said.

"Do you have a copy of it here somewhere???"

I said,
squinting at the stack of old CDs and video tapes under the TV.

"IMMA FIND IT NOW, I SWEAR!!!!"

I leant over the table, picked up the wine bottle and poured more wine into my glass barely making it inside the glass.
I continued to flip through my phone at the same time.

"DHEEP,"

he said sternly.

I flinched.

INSIDE VOICES MUCH?

"I don't like being interrupted,"

he said,
enunciating every letter.

MORTIFIED.

"I'm sorry, Ethan,"
I said.

Always in trouble.

Bloody Americans.

I placed the wine bottle back on the table, gently.

His hands
are clenched
into balls of rage.

He cupped one hand over the other fist and

cracked
his knuckles.

Oh, fucking fuck.

This isn't good.

"Are you s-u-re,"
he said, pausing to swallow,

"that you're q-u-i-t-e finished talking n-o-w?

Or
m-a-y
I
s-p-e-a-k?"

"I'm sure…
I'm sorry."
I said.

Fuck.

Who knows I'm here??

What the fuck is his fucking address??

Why the fuck don't I remember his fucking address??

I pressed my hands between my knees and try to sit still, patiently.
I stared at my knees.

He wasn't saying anything.

"I'm sorry, Ethan,"
I said.

Please continue,"
I said.

**"Now
are you s-u-r-e
you haven't got
a-n-y-t-h-i-ng else
you'd like to
i-n-t-e-r-r-u-p-t me
with?
D-h-e-e-p?"**

He tipped his chin at an angle

**<u>and I heard</u>
<u>the bones</u>**

in his
neck
click.

"I'm sure, Ethan.
I'm listening to you.
I'm sorry,"
I said.

Fuck.
Fuck.
Fuck.
Fuck.
Fuck.

How do I get his fucking address?

Need to get outta here.

"O-kay, good,"
he said,
staring off into the distance.

He sat back in his armchair and lit a cigarette.

"As I was saying…" he said.

I slid my hand over my phone.
I pulled it into my lap.

Eyes on him.
Eyes on him.

He's staring into space.

Good.

"And then we made it to number one in the Spanish charts," he said.

"That's AMAZING, wow! And what was that like?" I said.

"Well…"

I unlocked my phone and quickly typed a message to Jono.

What the fuck is his fucking address??

UBER!!

YES.

UBER!!!

GOD BLESS UBER!!!

Before I managed to press 'send' I was interrupted.

"DHEEP?"

He looks pissed.

Fuck Fuck Fuck Fuck.

"Sorry,"
I said.
"I was just texting my friend.

He was worried when
I didn't text him
back.

So, I just told him
I was here,

at your place."

Phew.

He took a puff of his cigarette and eyed me suspiciously.
I smiled and shifted in my seat.
He stubbed his cigarette in the ash tray, keeping his eyes on me.

"So,
you were saying,
about the tour?"
I said.

He stubbed the cigarette again,
watching it
as he slid it
around the rim
and
trapped it
in the centre.

He squinted at me.

"What's going on, Dheep?" he said.

"What do you mean?
I was just asking about your tour…"

"No. I mean, this."

He waved his hand at me,

**as if I should know
what
he was talking about.**

I looked away.

"'I d-o-n'-t know what you're talking about,
Ethan?"

"This.
This.
Whole…
Cold act?"

"Nothing.
It's nothing."

I fidgeted in my seat, drawing my legs up onto the sofa and leaning back against the cushions. I grabbed one and placed it in front of my knees.

"One minute it's all normal
and now…
this?"
he said.

My arms were tingling. Prickling my skin.

"I just…" I said.

"You just…?" he said.

He began rolling his hand, motioning me to speak.

"I just felt a little aggression back there…

that's all."

I watched my right thumb picking at my fingernails in my lap.

Hot and prickly,
all over.

"Agg-aggression?!"
he said.

"Umm...
Yeah…

just a little,"
I said.

He leaned his elbows on his knees and dropped his head into his hands.

He lifted his cap up and down with one hand as he combed his hair with his other hand.

He put his cap back on his head and sat up straight, with his fists clenched.

He stood up from the chair and walked around the table,

towards me.

I tried not to flinch.

Brace mode.

He's standing two feet away from me.

Watching me.

"Look at you,"

he said,
shaking his head,

"you're shaking."

He's still watching me.

Leering.

Watching me.

He turned and walked outside, to the balcony.

I watched him
stand over the glass railing,
looking out at the city.

He leaned over the edge,
resting,
smoking his cigarette.

I waited
and waited,
for him to come inside.

But he never did.

Waking up

I'm back in the
feline jungle.

Why is it so bright??

What is this leopard doing on me???

Shaking,
bubbling,
like a bottle of coke,
fallen on the granite floor.

**WHAT
IS
that pink
stuff again?**

Like
a firecracker,

waiting

to
explode.

Get me outta here.

Charlie.

No Versace.
No Gucci.

I look like shit.

Get outta here.

CC??

CC???

No phone,
No CC.

FUCK FUCK FUCK FUCK FUCK.

THE DOOR.

CHLOCK.

FUCK FUCK FUCK FUCK FUCK.

Hide.

I pulled the leopard over my head.

Footsteps?

Kitchen??

Fuck.
What do I do.

Complete silence.

Wait…

what is that…

on…

my

head? …

"AAAAH!!!"

I screamed,
shooting up
out of the blanket

and
slapping
my head
vigorously.

"AAAAH!!!"
"AAAAH!!!"
"AAAAH!!!"
"AAAAH!!!"

"Dheep??

DHEEP???"
Versace said.

The covers were off.

Sunlight.

I covered my face with both of my hands.

"Dheep, it's okay,"
Versace said.

"Don't come near me!"
I screamed, flinching, but refusing to move the grip of my hands on my face.

He's laughing.

I looked between my fingers.

He's sitting on his chair.

He's fucking laughing at me.

"It's only Gucci,"
he said.
"He just wanted
a cuddle, I guess."

Merp.

Dick move.

"Oh," I said.

"Dheep?"

"Yes."

"You can move your hands now."

I hesitated.

"No, I can't," I said.

"Why not?"

"I just…

I can't let you
see me
like this…"

I'm not wearing enough make-up.

He laughed harder.

"Too late,"
he said,
sounding more serious.

"I already took a picture
and posted it

on Instagram."

"YOU DID W-H-A-T??!"

I said, screaming and unintentionally moving my hands as I tried to get up.

He's laughing.

"You're joking?!" I said.

He's still laughing.

"I'm so fucking embarrassed," I said, covering my head with the leopard.

I felt the sofa dip.
Moving towards me.
Versace lay next to me and wrapped his arms around my shoulders, over the blanket.

"Don't be,"
he said.

"You're gorgeous."

"I'm still not coming out,"
I said.

**American boys.
FML.**

"That's fine with me," he said, gently stroking my head through the blanket.

"You can stay here as long as you like."

"Good… I will then."

"Good."

He kissed my head through the blanket.

"So…

do you want your pancakes under there as well?"

PANCAKES??

"Wh-where would we get pancakes from?" I asked.

"I ordered some,"
he said.
"They're in the kitchen."

"Kitchen?"
I said.

He's still stroking my head but now he's wrapped tighter around me.

"Yeah.

I didn't know
what you liked

so, I got
a little bit of everything.

Does that sound good?"

OMD.

"Umm…
yes,"
I said.

"Ummm… I just need to freshen up a little first…?"

He kissed the back of my head through the blanket again.

"Of course, go ahead."

"Okay…
could you,

ummm…

close your eyes please?"

He laughed softly.

"Okay," he said.

"'Starting now!"

"Okay!" he said.

"Are they closed??"

"YES YES, ma'am they're closed."

"Okay… where's CC?"

"She's over by the closet, next to your shoes."

"Okay, thank you…

Keep 'em CLOSED!"

"Yes ma'am, all closed."

I poked my head through the blanket and scoped the sitch.

I see CC.

En route.

Okay, I can do this.

I wobbled towards the closet.

I scooped up CC and beelined for the bathroom.

The following weekend

New York City,
the city with the
acrylic sunrise,
and everywhere else is
watercolour.

Borderline my best and worst time of day.

The time
Charlie's
well and truly
gone home
for the night.

Leaving us to pick up the pieces.
And get our sorry asses home.

WHY ARE YOU AWAKE AT THIS UNGOLDLY HOUR??

And

why

do you look so fresh
walking
your dogs??

Don't get me started on those fucking runners.

Not today though.

No Ubers for me.

I'm getting my
**tan
on.**

On Versace's balcony.

I took another puff.

Does it ever

drop below fifty degrees Celsius here??

We're somewhere between his first serious break-up and his childhood traumas.

His expression is glassy.

I think he's taking a break in the story because he's looking at me expectantly.

"Yeah, totally," I said.

He hesitated

and then continued on with his speech.

He looks like love on a stick.

A cheeky smile spread across his face.

"Whaa?" he said, giggling.

"So does that mean we're boyfriend and girlfriend now?"
I said.

Deadpan.

His cigarette fell into his lap.

One.

Two.

Three.

"Ah! Oh m-a-n!" he said.

Delayed reaction.

He flicked the cigarette off his lap.

"Wai- What did you?"

He said.

"I said…"

I reached over and put out my cigarette in the ash tray, on the table between us.
I glided over to him.

I perched myself in the crevice of his lap and dangled my legs over the arm rest.

I took off his cap and slipped it onto my head.

I looked deep into his eyes and said,

"I said…

does that mean
we're
boyfriend
and
girlfriend
now?"

Nothing.

I stared him dead in the eyes.

Still nothing.

The boy must be

deaf,

**dumb
and
blind.**

I put both my arms around his neck
and rested my head
on his nook.

He whispered into my hair,

"Yes."

As I lifted my head to look at him.

Our first kiss.

Meeting my therapist

"So, I haven't seen you for two weeks? Two weeks, is that right?"
Dr Hooberkoff said.

"Yesss, June 27th," I said.

"Okay... So, what's been going on?"

I have a boyfriend.

"Ummm...so there was fourth of July weekend..." I said.

"And how was that?"

"It was good...
I went on a boat..."

He looks impressed.

"And how was that?" he said.

"Good...
I made some new friends..."

"Well, isn't that

great
Dheep??"

"Yeah…
and…
I…uh…
I actually went to meet that guy
I told you about from…
umm…
Instagram?…
umm…"

"Ahh, yes
I r-e-m-e-m-b-e-r.

**He didn't reply
to your
message,
right?"**

Alright.

No need

for that, mate.

"Yeah…
Umm…
I'm not sure if I mentioned it before…
but I also met up with him…
uhh…
a couple of weeks
ago?…"

"Right, no, I don't think so."

"Oh… okay… so… a few of my friends and I went to his place to watch the fireworks…
and then I saw him again… this weekend just gone…"

"Oh-ka-a-y?" he said, fidgeting in his chair and looking bewildered.

Don't make me say it.

"Erm… and now… "

I looked into my lap and tried to get the words out.
I laughed nervously.

"Erm… and now…

we're in a relationship."

I peered up at him nervously.

You did say I should make new friends.

He chewed his lip.

"That's w-o-n-d-e-r-f-u-l news," he said, almost in a trance.

"I know it may seem a little out of the blue and it was all a little 'soon'…" I added quickly.

"Well how do you feel about it all?
Does it seem too soon to you?"

A little.

Maybe.

YES.

It seemed like a good idea at the time.

Charlie made me do it.

"Um, no not really...
I think it's something we both really want and we really like each other..."

"Okay, well that's great!"
He said.
"I wish you all the best together!"

????

"So, tell me? What is it that you like about him?" he said.

Oh, fucking drop it already.

"What do I like about him?" I said, buying time and pondering out the window.

He nodded.

I haven't got a fucking clue.

"He's like my best friend…"
I said.

"We just talk for hours and hours, all night long…

He's like my best friend…
I can tell him anything…

I mean, I know that sounds clich ..."

He continued nodding his head like Churchill.

"That all sounds great, Dheep," he said, smiling and looking at the clock.

"But that's all we have time for today."

Wonderful.

I'm so glad we had this talk.

We're supposed to be having Fi over for dinner

"Sorry, honey, we're running a bit late. We're just popping into a bar to see some friends on the way. You wanna come meet us there instead?"

Sent.
To Versace.
02:04 am.

Fi cut three more lines of Charlie on the dresser.

"Fi, shouldn't we just go straight to Versace's? We're supposed to be having dinner, remember?"

"Babe, yeah just chill…
we'll be there soon.
I said we'd swing by Ricky's bar first.

It'll only take a minute."

"Come on, Fi…
I feel b-a-d,

he's been waiting for us

for hours…"

She passed me the straw.

"Another one,"
I said, sniffing.
"I need to sober up."

Fi looked over at Kev, for permission.

He looked at me with disdain.
And nodded at Fi.

Calm down.
I'm not gonna rob your shit.

Fi emptied the bag and handed me her straw and card.

"Right, I'm out."
I said.

I waved to Kev, hugged Fi and picked up my overnight bag.

"Do what you gotta do, babe," she said, waving me off.

Outside Versace's apartment

Locked.

Strange.

He normally leaves it open for me.

I rang the bell.

No answer.

I rang again.

Nothing.

CHLOCK.

The door opened.

Versace standing in front of me, avoiding eye contact.

His eyes look red and puffy.

He doesn't look pleased.

"I'm SO SORRY, babe!"

I said, flinging my arms around his neck and kissing his cheek.

Cold as stone.

I walked passed him into the lounge area. I hooked my bag and coat over one of the chairs and continued on.
"Fi came over,
then we got talking for longer than I expected…

you know how it is…

I'm really sorry we couldn't do dinner this time…"

I stopped in my tracks.

Noah's ark.

The entire table was filled with trays and trays, tiers and tiers of food.

Versace.

Gold trays.

Gold plates.

Gold cutlery.

Gold tea set.

Versace.

Fuck.

My.

Life.

"It's cold,"
he said

as he stormed past me and outside to the balcony.

Fuck.

My.

Life.

His back to the apartment,
leaning against the edge,
in his favourite spot,
smoking a cigarette
and staring out at the city.

"I'm in trouble, Gucci."

I went to the bathroom.

Charlie.

Sober up.

He's not moved.

I moved up behind him and tried to wrap my arms around his waist.

He shrugged me off without looking at me.

He walked away and sat on his chair. He pulled down his cap, so I couldn't see his face. He wiped his face with the back of his hand.

I picked up my chair from the other side of the balcony and placed it opposite his.

I sat down, lent forward and rested my hands, palms down on his knees.

"What do you want?" he asked.

"I want you," I said, innocently.

"What exactly do you want from me?"

"I don't know what you mean."

He glared at me.

"Where were you tonight?"

My lips wouldn't speak.

"And don't tell me

you were at home."

Fuck.

"I never said I was at home, Ethan…"

"Are you fucking kidding me?!

You're gonna

lie to me, now?"

He swatted my hand from his knee and stood up, stomping his feet. I quickly flung my arms round his neck.

"WAIT! Please don't go!!"

He ducked out of my grip and moved past me.

"WAIT!"

I cried, pulling him back to the seat.

"Let me explain… please…"

He looked at me with disgust.

He sat down, refusing to look at me.

"I know it's gonna sound bad…"

He stood up again.

"WAIT!"

I pleaded, pulling him back down.
"Just let me finish… please?.."

He sat down again.
I put my head face-down on his knee.

"I was with Fi and her friend…" I said.

"What friend?"

"Her friend…
who is a guy…"

He pushed my head away and stood up again.

I wrestled him back to the chair and sat astride his lap, pinning his shoulders down.

"But it's NOT LIKE THAT…
I promise, Ethan!…"

I started wailing crying.

"Don't.
I don't need your crocodile tears,"
he said, breaking my grip on his shoulders.

"WE WERE DOING LINES, OKAY?!!"
I screamed.

"You expect me to believe that?" he said, sounding insulted.

"No… I mean, yes…

he's just an OLD MAN that's all…

One of her STUPID friends…

I didn't even know that's where we were going,

I thought we **WERE** going to the bar!!"

He lifted my head gently from underneath my chin and looked me dead in the eyes.

**"Where.
Were.**

You?"

"In a hotel room," I blurted.

"I can't."

He gently rolled me off of him and walked back to the edge of the balcony.

I sat on the floor,
curled over my knees,
staring at the tiny hairs
on my legs.

"It…
w-a-s-n't…
like that…

I
s-w-e-a-r
Ethan…

<u>I only have eyes for you."</u>

"SO WHY ARE YOU TURNING UP HERE AT THREE AM EVERY NIGHT, DRUNK AND OUT OF YOUR MIND?!!"
he yelled.

"Because I'm fucked up?"
I said, sounding like a petulant child.

"This is New York City. **<u>RAIN CHECK.</u>** <u>**We're all fucked up.**</u> Why are you any different?"

"Because…"

"BECAUSE WHAT??"

"BECAUSE!!!"
I screamed and sprang up to face him.

"BECAUSE I WANT TO D-I-E EVERY DAY!!"

Fuck.
Why did I just say that.

"What?"

"Nothing.
Never mind."

The emotion drained from his face.
He took a step closer.

"Show me."
He said.

"Show you what?"
I said, taking a step back.

"SHOW ME,"

he said louder, taking another step.

"I don't know what you're talking about!"

He took a step closer and pulled my wrists.

"Show me,"

he said again.

He overpowered me and ripped the watch from my wrist.

"Oh fuck,"

he said, suddenly letting go.

He swung around and leaned right over the edge, covering his face with his cap.
I crawled around for my watch and tried to put it back on.
Shaking too much.
Replaced the Band-Aid

and began
to silently
cry
into
my hair.

Don't leave.

An eternity.

**Digging my nails
into my arm.**

I want to go home.

Fingers touched my shoulder.

**Pulled me,
rolled me,**

into his heart.

The next morning

He's out cold.

I lifted up the covers and slid out. I tip-toed to the bathroom with CC.

Charlie.

Don't.

Don't even.

I can't deal with your shit today.

I went out to the balcony.

Cold air.

Cigarette.

Tastes like shit.

Look at them,

**just going about
their daily business,**

day in,

day out.

What the fuck are we doing here.

The sound of a door opening.

"Good morning," he said soberly.

He handed me his Nirvana hoodie.

I put it on.

He sat down in the corner of the balcony,

watching me.

Pity.

Fear.

What have I done.

He's wearing last night's clothes.

He lit up a cigarette, careful not to look at me.

I sat down on the opposite side of the balcony.

His chair.

I hooked my knees up and rested my feet on the edge of my chair opposite.

It's still there.

He hasn't moved it yet.

"Come inside,"
he said,
standing by the door and beckoning my inside.
"I'll order us some pancakes."

I curled up on the edge of the sofa, biting onto a cushion. Gucci watching me curiously from the other end of the sofa.

He hates me now.

Versace gently placed something on the table.

A plate.

Charlie.

"Go for it," he said calmly.

I observed his body language, trying to understand.

He walked back over to the kitchen and fired up the kettle.

I stared at the plate, without moving.

"It's okay,"
he said.

He came and sat down in the chair opposite.
He leaned forward, his fingers locked in a steeple.

"No judgement,"
he said.

Nervous,
I pulled the plate over

and inhaled.

He walked back over to the kitchen to make tea.

Monday morning and my alarm is going off

Snooze.
Snooze.
Snooze.
Snooze.
Snooze.
Snooze.

Thwack.

"Oh, shit.
Sorry, Ethan!"

I forgot he was there.

"That's okay," he said rubbing his nose. "I was just getting up."

"It's five AM. You don't have to get up…"

"I want to."

He butterfly kissed me on the head three times, whipped off the covers and jumped out of the bed.

Christ.

Morning people.
FML.

I rolled back under the duvet, pulling it all the way over my head.

Now I'll have to get up.

What is he doing to me.

I still have 10 more snoozes to go.

"Honey, are you getting in the shower?" he asked.

I hate you.

I rolled over.

Pretend not to hear.

"It's nearly five thirty. Won't you be late?"

What
the
actual
fucking

fuck.

Leave
me
the fuck
alone.

"YES, HONEY!" I yelled politely, kicking off the covers.

"THANK YOU, for reminding me honey!"

Why are you ruining my life.

I sat on the edge of the bed and groaned.
I rubbed my eyes and stood up.
I then shuffled over to the bathroom with my head hunched over like a zombie.

Thirty minutes later.

Dressed, make-up on, hair soaking wet and not even combed through.

Charlie.

Ready.

I opened the bathroom door to a

**very
perky**
Versace.

He's like a sunrise

in the middle of an apocalypse.

"You
Are
GORGEOUS,"
he said dreamily.

**I look
like
a drowned**

rat.

"Here,"
he said.
"I made you this."

He presented me with a plate of scrambled eggs, with a fork and knife.

"It's all I could find,"
he said.

I thanked him
and forced the
whole
plate
down.

Shit.

I got those months ago.

That evening

"Three one eight?" The doorman said.

"Yes?"

"You have a delivery.
A gentleman hand-delivered this for you this morning."

He smiled at me.

A delivery?
From a gentleman?

He disappeared behind the desk and re-emerged, carrying a large white, drawstring bag in one hand and a **huge** pink and white Orchid plant in the other.

It's almost as tall as him.

"Are you sure that's for three one eight??" I said.

"Yes, ma'am."

The Orchid received pride of place, right in the centre of the breakfast bar.
The only decoration in the whole place.

My favourite.

I sat down at the coffee table.
I carefully unravelled the gold ribbon.

Item one.
A keratin-based shampoo made with natural ingredients. Looks expensive.

Someone's calling my phone.
Jono.

"Hey Jono, what's up?"

"He-e-y, I'm just in the neighbourhood and thought I'd come say hey, but I've only got like an hour because I have to get back to Brooklyn for a date… Wanna hang?"

"Yeah, come over, I just got back from therapy."

"Cool, I'm with the doorman. Buzz me up?"

"Sure thing… see you in a sec."

The door phone buzzed.

"Hello Dheep. We have a JONO here for you?" The doorman said.

"Sure, just buzz him up, thank you!"

We kissed each cheek.

"H-e-e-y girl!
Ooooooooh!
New orchids??"

"Yep!"

"Versace?"

"I'm about to find out… Come look."

"I got these too… HAND delivered by a gentleman, according to the doorman…"

"Ooooh!" Jono said, his eyes lighting up.

He picked up the shampoo and gasped.

"OH MY GOSH! This stuff is supposed to be AMAZING! … It's like REALLY EXPENSIVE!

I hate you right now."

He shook his head and sat down, huffing.

"Well you're welcome to borrow some anytime," I said.

He smiled.

"What else is there?" he said, pulling the bag towards him and looking inside.

"HE-E-Y!! GIMME A CHANCE, will you??"

I pulled the bag away from him and sat down next to him.

"That stuff in there looks really expensive… is this stuff all from Versace?"

I shrugged my shoulders and winked at him.

"I don't know yet… I'm saving the card for last,"

He rolled his eyes and slumped back in the seat.

"You… WOULD."

We looked through the bag together, carefully studying all the items.

Item two.
Hair styling serum.

Items three to six.
Dr. Hauschka cleansing milk.

Dr. Hauschka clarifying toner.
Dr. Hauschka Creme Purifiante.
Dr. Hauschka eye serum.

Item seven.
Organic toothpaste.
Random.

Item eight.
Q-tips.
Also, random.

Item nine.
A natural body wash that smelled divine.

"These are really random gifts, Dheep," Jono said.

He's sampled everything except the Q-tips.

"I think it's really sweet," I said, coo-ing.

He rolled his eyes again.

"You would."

I stuck my tongue out at him.

I reached for the card.

Nothing written on the front.
Just plain, gold, with no lettering.

I opened the card.

Inside, the letters were perfectly aligned and written in all caps.

It read:

"MY PRINCESS, MY QUEEN,

HERE IS JUST A LITTLE SOMETHING I PICKED UP FOR YOU WHILE I WAS OUT TODAY. ALWAYS THINKING OF YOU! YOU ARE MY WORLD!

ETHAN -
xoxoxoxoxo"

Next to his name was a little heart.

"YUK!"
Jono said.

He stuck his fingers down his throat and pretended to vom.

I was just about to go to bed when Versace called

FaceTime…

Are we still doing this.

Really.

I've already removed my make-up.

FFS.

I pulled the hairband out of my bun and pulled my hair down over and around my face.

Lighting.

I sat on the corner of the sofa, near to the window.
It was darker there.
I lit a cigarette and answered.

"H-e-e-y gorgeous,"
he said, waving.

He's on the balcony, wearing a Bulls cap.

"Hiya,"
I said, waving back.

"I can't see you, move into the light."

FF-.

I shifted to the other side of the sofa, trying to find a good angle.

"How was your day, honey?" he said.

"It was hard… but it's better now… Thank you for asking."

"How was yours?" I said.

"It was g-o-o-d… just making some beats here with Gucci."

He flipped the screen to Gucci who was laying on the floor, presenting his cute little butt,
like he does.
He poised his head towards the camera.

"Hi G-u-c-c-i!"
I said, waving.

Versace reappeared.

"I worry about you," he said, sounding serious.

"Why?" I laughed.

His eyes are salty.

"What's wrong?" I said, confused.

He wiped his eyes and looked away.
He sniffed, shook his head and turned back towards the camera.

"You can't even look at yourself, can you?" he said.

"What do you mean?" I asked, worried and confused.

"Do you even like yourself?"

he said.

Where is all this coming from??

"Yeah, sure… I have no real complaints…" I said, a little bothered.

"Have you thought any more about…

seeing a psychiatrist…

like we said on Sunday?"

No.

"I already have a therapist, Ethan? … What is this about?…"

"I think…

it may help…

to see a good psychiatrist as well,
who can maybe prescribe something…

you know there are loads of **great doctors out there now**

and they have these **great new medications**.

you won't even feel a thing,

there's very little side effects…"

Exactly.
I won't feel a thing.

"Let me stop you there, Ethan…"

I'm fine.

"I'll look into it tomorrow, okay?" I said.

"Sure. Good," he said.

He studied me again for a second.

"Send me a picture of your insurance card. I can book an appointment for you…
I do this all the time for my boss,"
he said.

"Okay…
Thank you,"
I said.

"Okay."

He smiled and blew me a kiss.

"I'm gonna go now… you get some rest, beautiful!" he said.

"Okay, honey… goodnight."

"Goodnight."

Chapter Five: Love

There's a war in my mind

Charlie has been my friend for so long now. I couldn't imagine a life without him,
 by my side.

No problem too small.

No wound too deep.

I remember when my best friend left the city.

It was her time.

She escaped.

I didn't see it that way at the time, but she did escape.

I asked Chloe what she did, when she moved to London for a two-year work assignment.

"Oh, I flew home nearly every weekend…
my boyfriend was in New York,"
she said.

"Oh,"
I said.
"Right."

"And what about the times you didn't fly home."

"I used to hang out with friends from work or friends I knew living in the city at the time."

"Oh,"
I said.
"Right."

"That's nice,"
I said.

"It's nice you had someone."

"Oh, actually…"
she said.

"Yeah?"

"Sometimes I used to just walk around the city for hours just to get to know the different neighbourhoods, when I was looking for a place to live."

I did that once.

I walked from Meatpacking to Midtown.

I'm not much of a 'walker',
but I thought I'd try it out.

Note to self:
Four inch
heels
are not
walking shoes.

Also note to self:
<u>Stop using
Sex and The City
as a tour guide.</u>

Also also note to self:

**At least
fucking
wear tights
next time.**

There are a lot of people out on the streets today.

Everyone has someone.

I give up.

I'm going home.

Just as I began to retreat in a zombie-like state back to my temporary abode, I felt someone calling out to me.

"Hey, miss!"
A voice yelled from behind me.

I stopped and turned around.

A homeless person.
How rude of me.
I reached into my pocket for some change.

"Miss, you dropped something back there," he said.

He smiled and gestured in the direction I had walked from.

Apprehensive, I pressed my bag against my thigh.

It's a busy enough street?

"Thank you," I said. "What did I drop?"

He took his hand out of his pocket and rested it on his chest.

I felt for my phone in my left pocket and tried to remain still.

"MY HEART."

He said.

<u>Well, thank fuck for that.</u>

I relaxed my grip on my bag, blew him a kiss and giggled, all coy-like.

It was then I realised he wasn't homeless after all.

I think he's on his way to the gym.

I skipped off, into the distance, smirking all the way.

"HEY MISS?.... " I heard him yell.

"CAN I HAVE YOUR NUMBER AT LEAST??"

I looked briefly over my shoulder, all smiles, and waved at him before I turned and went on my merry way.

I spent nearly 20 years hiding my face.

Utterly ridiculous
now I think about it.

There's always something isn't there?

Something we're trying to hide,
trying to conceal,

**or
just wish
would go
and take a
running leap
off our faces.**

I got mine from my dad.
You think he might have warned me?
Or at least have discovered a cure by now?

And everyone tries to tell you,

**"It doesn't really matter
 in the grand scheme of things."**

or my favourite,

"No-one can notice it but you."

Yadda yadda yadda…

That's a

big,

ugly,

load of bollocks,

isn't it??

Back to present day:
There's a war in my mind

There's a war in my mind,
and it's been there some time.

But I'd be lying if I said I wasn't sick of it.

When I met Charlie, everything changed for me, here in New York City.

It was right around the time I decided to drop-kick the memories of my ex to the curb,

I just thought,

fuck it.

What else is there?

I was sick of it.

Day in,
day out.

Same shit, different day.

Nothing ever changes.

I found Charlie, and he found me.

Night after night,
day after day.

JJ has her hook-ups.
So does Jono.
Fi has…

well all the same things as me, really.

Champagne, Charlie and cigarettes.

The 3 C's.

But there are times even I, wish he'd give me a break every now and then.

Charlie, that is.

That's usually around 4am on a school night,
when I realise I have work in a few hours
and I'm still washing down
a few lines of Charlie
with whatever alcohol
is kicking around
the apartment.

Fuck my life.

It'd be nice to

be with someone,

you know?

Cue Versace

Versace wasn't like **the others.**

He stuck around for longer than a New York minute, for a start.

He doesn't seem to give

a flying fuck
what
I do,

half the time.

Sometimes I would do things just to annoy him.

Just to see.

I stopped wearing make-up around the house when we were alone, on days

when monsters were literally eating off my face.

I threw my hair up in a mess and didn't shower all day.

I wore all of his clothes and sent him to the store to get coffee in the early hours of the morning,

**because I couldn't possibly
be seen like this
in public.**

**I incessantly asked him
stupid questions
all day long
about**

**why he was doing
whatever he was doing**

and could he

please take a break

to make me some tea.

If he was bothered, he never showed it.

He smiled and just said,

"Yes, honey."

"Whatever you want, honey."

"Is there anything else my princess wants, honey?"

Dumbfounded.

Twenty-one days.

Twenty-one days to break a habit,
my mother said.

Twenty-one days.

It's not long is it, really?

So, I told him,
Versace:

"I'm going to give up Charlie for twenty-one days."

And that was that.

I'm giving up Charlie for twenty-one days

Versace shrugged his shoulders.

"Up to you,"
he said.

"No difference to me."

Weird.

This has to be some reverse psychology, no?

He doesn't seem that smart.

"Day 1,"
I sent him in a text message at work.

"Just 21 days.
I can do this."

Ten minutes later.

"Versace, I can't do this.

Today is **SO HARD.**

I just hate everyone and everything…

I just need a little help.

Please?"

His reply:

"I'm not stopping you.

You can do what you want.

I told you.

No difference to me."

Okay, sooooo…

what the fuck is this?

That could have been a test
and you would have failed miserably.

But it isn't.

I fucking need Charlie,
God help me,
man alive,
I need it.

"Whatever you need.

No difference to me,"

he said.

What the -

Fuck it,
I don't really know what to do here.

So, I stuck it out.

Note to self:
Next time,
leave the fucking Charlie at home.

Later that night

As I walked through the door to my apartment, I stuffed Charlie back into the top kitchen drawer and marched over to the TV area.

As I sat there and switched the TV on, I looked over at Charlie.

Alone.

In the kitchen drawer.

Couldn't hurt? ...

It's been a long day...

A reward....

after a long day.

I got up.
And sat back down.
I got up.
And sat back down.

Fuck it.

I ran over to Charlie.
And rescued him from his prison.

I grabbed the bag and ran back to the dresser, which houses the TV.
I flung the contents over onto the dresser haphazardly.

DDDZZZZZZZ.

Fuck.

The buzzer.

Charlie exploded all over the dresser, and down the sides onto the floor.

Shit.

I ran over to the phone.

"Hello?" I said.

"Miss Dheep,

we have an ETHAN BANNER here to see you."

HOLY FUCK.

"Sure, send him up," I said, coolly.

I stared at the snow mountain over by the TV.
No time.

I ran over with the straw.

Should I?

I looked at the floor and the sides of the dresser.

Looks like Nigella exploded up in here.

No time no time no time.

Knock knock.

Holy cow.

I grabbed a paper towel and soaked it in water.
I quickly used it to mop up the floor and the sides of the dresser.

I grabbed a lone birthday card hanging around nearby.

Thanks, sis.

Knock knock.

"Yeah, I'm just coming!" I yelled.

I scooped the mountain into the birthday card and gently placed it in the top drawer with my undies.

All clear.

I ran back to the kitchen, threw away the towel and answered the door.

"Hi Ethan...

I wasn't expecting you here tonight?"

We need to talk about these surprise visits.

"I know,"
he said moving past me and into the apartment.

He looked around the room.

"I thought I'd surprise you,"
he said.

He pulled me in to his arms and kissed me.
I squeezed him back.

So warm.

"Come on,"
he said, with his hands now on my shoulders, gently pushing me away.

"Get your things.

I'm
taking you
shopping."

S-H-O-P-P-I-N-G???

"Shopping??"
I said, trying not to seem overly excited.

"Yeah," he said.

He walked over to the fridge, bent over and looked inside.

"We need to get you some food."

Oh.

Food shopping.

I'll sound the trumpets.

Going food shopping

"You'll need this,"
Versace said, placing a bottle of organic apple juice into the shopping cart.

"I - ... I don't drink sugary drinks..."

"And this."

He placed a bottle or organic orange juice into the shopping cart, next to the apple juice.

"And this...
and this...
and this..."

He piled more and more and more juices and smoothies into the cart.

"Versace!"

I yelled.

He glowered at me.

I lowered my voice.

"Sorry..."

I said,
"but I don't think I really need all this stuff…"

I've never even used the kitchen before.

I use the freezer to store my jeans.

Or to clean my gym kit overnight.

What is he even thinking??

He pulled me into him and kissed me on the forehead, turning me to face him.

"Just trust me, okay?"

I nodded slowly, apprehensive.
I handed him back the juice.

He placed in back in the cart and wheeled it along to the next section.

The shopping cart was full to the brim.

He's still going.

What the fuck
is a beef fillet??

Am I meant to stick that in the oven??
Or in the microwave??

He's totally overestimating my abilities here.

"You'll like this,"
he said, picking up something that looked like a cross between a potato and a carrot.

You said that twenty items ago.

And twenty before that.

We're waiting in line at the registers.

Who exactly is paying for all this shit??

My fury
was interrupted
by a grape
flying directly at my face.

It bounced off my nose
and nosedived
down my dress.

Versace.

<u>Oh, you think that's funny, do you?</u>

It's on.

I abandoned the shopping cart and chased him around the shop floor.

He's in the bread aisle.

I managed to corner him at the end of the aisle, dive bombing him into a carefully constructed pyramid of

natural,
organic,
preservative-free,
vitamin A-and-protein-enriched
bread.

I climbed on top him, pinning him against the rubble of bread, splaying across the floor.

"No! Get off me!"

He protested through laughter.

"Uhh..
Miss?...
Sir?..."

I heard a voice behind me calling.

"MISS?!

You need to get up from there!"

I pulled the grape out from my dress and brought it to his lips. He was trying to swat me away, choking through his laughter.

"Ahahahah!
STOP!
STOP DHEEP!
S-T-O-P!
We're gonna get kicked -"

"MISS?!"

I felt a hand tapping on my shoulder.

"Sorry sir,"
I said.

"We just had a bit of an accident,"
I said, as he pulled me up by my elbow.

We scurried away, back to our abandoned cart, which was miraculously still there and waiting patiently in line.

He said,

**"DAYUM girl!
You're gonna get us in trub -"**

I stuffed the grape into his mouth.

"Trouble?"
I said, smiling menacingly.

He pretended to be offended.
He chewed the grape and swallowed it down.

**"That'll be
three hundred,
thirty-four dollars
and fifty-nine cents,
please,"**

the girl at the register said.

I searched for my wallet.

**Thank you,
Versace.**

"Thank you, sir,"
she said.

I looked up.
Versace was typing in his pin.

"Umm… Thank you, Versace."

He carried my bags all the way home,
in silence.

"Are you sure I can't carry one of those?"
I asked, for once actually genuinely expecting to take at least one.

"Nope,"
he said.

His face looks flushed.
The hair under his cap is glistening.
He has four bags hanging from each shoulder,

including one hanging around his neck
and swaying slightly in front of his chest
and one strapped over his back.

I lit a cigarette for him and held it to his lips at each crossing.

Several women gawped
as they walked past.

Does he see them?

He's wearing sunglasses.
I can't tell.

What does he want from me??

"I wouldn't want you to break a nail,"
he said.

He really means it.

I had my nails done the other day.

"I liked the other shape better,"
he said.

"The coffin one.
That was cool…

You should get some in gold next time."

<u>So, I did.</u>

I received hundreds of compliments that week.

Ivy must've had a field day.

When we got back to the apartment he told me to sit down.

"You relax, honey… I got this."

He put the beef fillet in the oven and worked away.

I lay on the sofa,
wrapped in a cocoon
of blankets

occasionally looking over at Netflix.

I watched him carefully unload each bag, one item at a time, placing each one on the counter and then moving them around into neat piles for 'fridge' food, 'freezer' food and 'cupboard' food.
He turned them so the labels were all facing forward.
Like a football game.

His eyes scrunched up as he pondered over each one.

He placed each of the 'fridge' items in the fridge, one by one,

spacing them
exactly one inch
away from the edge.

With two fingers in between.

Grouped only with 'their kind'.

It was refrigerator art.

When dinner was ready, he served me up a plate and put the rest away in the fridge.

Then he kissed me goodbye and went home.

Day six without Charlie.

My head feels clammy.

Am I getting sick?

I can't make any conversation tonight.

Too much.

Silence.

Please.

**"It's okay, honey.
Go chill and watch Netflix,"**
he said, gesturing me towards the sofa.

"Thank you…"
I said.

I wrapped myself in the cocoon of blankets and rested my head

on the pile of cushions,
while he made the dinner.

Close your eyes.

It will all be fine.

Everything hurts.

I noticed a flash of something over by Versace, behind the breakfast bar.

He's holding a bouquet of red roses.

Where did he find a bouquet of red roses??

"Hey, pretty lady,"
he said.

"What do you have there?"
I asked, curious.

He carefully placed another stem into the bouquet, checking and adjusting his choice of location.

He held it out in front of him, twisting it around, in different angles.
Checking.

Checking.
Checking.

He watched me, watching him.

He winked at me.

Then he clutched the bouquet towards his chest

**and hummed
the wedding march,**

swaying side to side.

"Just for you,"
he said,

"It's to make you smile."

He blew me an air kiss and continued preening.

Day seven without Charlie

Fuck,
I'm late for work.

I was nearly out the door.

"Honey?"
Versace said.

What's he doing in the closet??

"Yes, honey?"
I said, sweetly.

"Do you mind if I send these to be fixed?"
he said, holding up a few of my work dresses.

"Fixed? What do you mean?"

"Well, the seam is ripped on this one,"
he said waving my black dress from out of the closet.

I've been meaning to get that fixed…

"Okay…"

"And this one has a coffee stain on it..."
He said, now holding out my favourite black and white pin-striped dress I wear to work nearly every week.

How long has that been there…

"Actually, I might just send them all to my tailor."

"Okay,"
I said.
"Just don't go to any trouble?"

I'm late for work.

"It's no trouble, babe,"
he shouted.

"Okay,"
I said.
"Do whatever you think."

I'm late for work.

"The whole place could do with some organizing,"
he said.
"Is that okay?"

I'm late for work.

"Only if it's not too much trouble?"
I said.

He poked his head out the side of the closet door.

"No, of c-o-u-r-se not,"
he said.
"This is what I do!"

Note to self:
Find out what it is that you do for a living again.

I'm late for work.

"Okay then,"
I said.
"YES PLEASE! ...
I gotta go now though, babe!"

I'm really late for work.

I blew him a kiss and scarpered out the door.

Coming home from work: Day seven without Charlie

UGHHHHHH!!

Where the FUCK are my FUCKING KEYS again??

I threw my bag onto the floor and kicked it.

Why is everything so hard all the time??

I tipped the bag upside down.

Lipstick, make-up brushes and tampons rolled down the corridor, stopping only for the walls.

I fucking hate my life.

There,
the first place I checked.

I buried my face in the palm of my hands.

One... two... three... four...

ten.

Let's go.
I scraped my things from the floor and swept them back inside. I grabbed hold of the wall behind me and slid myself up carefully. I pushed the key inside the door and walked inside.

I don't want to be here.

I hurled my bag and keys onto the counter.
The kitchen drawer.

Charlie.

No.

I went to pour myself some wine instead.

Something's not right.

I stopped dead in the centre of the room, staring ahead at the window sill.

What the fuck.

I looked at the other window sill next to the bed.

What the fuck.

I looked around the room, at all the walls and surfaces.

What the fuck is he doing??

I covered my mouth with my hands.

I dropped to my knees and cried, sobbing shamelessly into my hands.

He's only gone and

<u>redecorated the whole place.</u>

The walls were full with frame after frame, filled with happy smiles and laughter.

A collage of picture frames - me in Miami, surrounded by an army of all my long-lost childhood friends from back home.

It's like something out of Crate and Barrel in here.

He's given me his bedding?

Why?

Gorgeous furs.
Silks.
Cushions.
Throws.

Candles.

I have candles.

I took a deep breath in as I opened the door to the closet.

Oh.

It's the same.

It does look a bit cleaner in here though...

And I see half of my dresses are now gone.

What am I going to wear to work??

Why has he done this??

I walked into the bathroom to wipe my eyes.

This too??

I never seen a bathroom look so good.

I have a shower curtain!!

And it's CLEAN!!

I opened the bathroom cabinet, disguised by the large mirror.

Oh holy -

Cabinet art.

I dropped to my knees again.

I lay,
sprawled across the floor,
sobbing into my hair.

Day ten without Charlie.

Shit,
I'm fucking late
again.

    I gulped down the remains of the vino and ushered Jono out the door.

"Shit, I'm so fucking late!"
I said, as we tried to flag a cab.

I passed the cigarette to Jono.
I answered the phone,

"I'm so sorry honey,
I'm just waiting for a cab now…

yep…
I tried…

surge pricing….

Okay, cool,
thank you…

see you soon.

Bye!"

Fuck,
I'm so drunk.

I need to sober up.

Charlie Charlie Charlie.

The rest of the night was a blur.

A big fat,
ugly,
messy
blur.

I can't make out his features,
but I know he's there.

Champagne.

More champagne.

I've waited months to eat at Buddakan…

Versace is quiet tonight.

Something's not right.

"Dheep,

I've been meaning to talk to you about something."

Fuck, not good.

More champagne.

"Sure, what is it?"
I said,
trying to enunciate like an adult.

I reached over and put my hand somewhere over his.

Stop shaking.
Keep still.

"Ah… um…"

he said.

I hear him coughing.

He's making me nervous.

What's going on?

"Here are your drinks,"
the waiter said

I swiped the glass of champagne and lifted the glass.

"Chin chin!"

Fuck,
I need Charlie.

Versace took a sip of his drink.
He gently pulled my hands towards his, forcing me to release the glass.

"Dheep… I uh…"

I squeezed his hand gently,
urging him to get to the point.

Fuck,
I need Charlie.

How did I get so drunk?

The room was spinning around and around, and it was taking everything in me,

to not vomit
all over the table.

Get to the point, Versace.

"Sometimes
you may not know someone
for very long
but…"
he said.

My skin feels cold.
Clammy.
Fish-like.

Get to the point, Versace.

The sweats.

I'm going to be sick.

I squeezed his hand gently and leaned closer.
I tapped his hand, reassuringly.

Get to the point, Versace.

<u>Before I vom all over your nice coat.</u>

"My mum said…
that you don't
really
know
someone,
until…"

Get to the point, Versace.

I squeezed his hand again.

I can feel it coming up.

"I love you too."

I said.

He gawped at me.

I waited.

"I said…"

He kissed the top of my hand.

"I love you, Dheep."

I returned his smile and kissed his hands too.

Good, because now

I'm going to throw up.

I excused myself and ran to the bathroom.

Chapter Six: Descent

Day twelve without Charlie.

"Here,
take this,"

Versace said.

"It might
help
with the
cravings."

Versace handed me a blue pill.

Methamphetamine.

You may know it as it's street name.

Adderall.

☐ **Meet Adderall** ☐

Adderall, for those of you who don't know,

is like
the wonder drug
that gives
Bradley Cooper his

'super powers'

in Limitless.

It's also conveniently available on prescription from any reputable psychiatrist.

And, if you're struggling to get a prescription there, just get onto your local drug dealer.

The first time I met Adam

- that's Adderall to you -

was a regular day in the office,
before I even met Charlie.

It was no unusual morning at the water cooler, you could say.

I had Hangover Brain.

So, I was busy stockpiling on coffee, sweets and, regrettably, H2O.

"Here, take this,"

Christopher said.

A phrase I would become **very** accustomed to, during my life in New York City.

"Thanks,"
I said.

With hesitation, I eventually replied,

"What is it?"

Christopher gave me one of those,

'You can thank me later'

smirks
that only douchebags wear.

"It'll sort your hangover right out!"
He said.

Douchebag smile.

Douchebag wink.

Douchebag gun-like motion to complete the douchebag toolkit.

"It'll be your most productive day ever!"
He added, as he turned and walked away.

**Then
this
dickhead
went
and
ate
it.**

He was right about two things though, I'll give him that.

Back to Versace:
Day twelve without Charlie.

"Here,
take this,"

Versace said.

"It might
help
with the
cravings."

Don't mind if I do.

Update:

1. The 21 days are up.
And then some.

Officially divorced Charlie

2. Have replaced Charlie with Adam.

Now commencing love affair that tops all love affairs

3. And drinking heavily at almost every opportunity.

Much to Versace's disagreement

4. Have, however,

decided to lift
7-year ban

on
carbs,
sugar,
fizzy drinks
and junk food.

Pretty much winning all around

Meeting with my therapist

"Tell me more about that,"
Dr Hooberkoff.

"How does it feel to want to die every day?"

"How does it feel?"
I asked.

"Yes."
He said.
"What does it **feel** like?"

It feels like I want to die every day.

"I don't really know,"
I said, playing with my fingers as I spoke.

Dr Hooberkoff shifted uncomfortably in his chair.

Sympathetic face.

"Oh-kay,"
he said, bringing his fingers to his lips.

"Let's try this another way...
Talk me through

when you get this feeling and
what thoughts are going through your mind at the time."

Listening face.

"Oh-kay…

So, for example, today…
I've just got my toast and coffee from the canteen at work
and I'm walking back to the elevator to go back to my desk
and all I think is,

'I want to die, I want to die'

and just
every minute
of the day

feels

like pure torture…

How's that?"

He stared at me and gulped loudly.

Reset.

Game face.

"When you say you get this **feeling** that you want to **die**,

can you explain that feeling a little bit more?

Is it a **numb feeling**

or are there any **emotions** going on in your mind at the time?"

"There are no feelings.

Just a voice,

my voice,

telling me
I want to die.

**And
every
day
feels
like
pure
torture."**

You need a hobby

"You need a hobby."

"You need a hobby," Versace said.

Don't fucking tell me I need a HOBBY.

Maybe **drinking** **is** my HOBBY,

"I have a hobby,"
I said.

"I write."

"Great!"
Versace said.

"What are you writing?"

"I'm writing an expose on the benefits **of abusing Adam.**"

I spent the next hour,
on the balcony,
in the middle of a monsoon,
chaining cigarettes,
guzzling Pepsi,
and chasing down Adam,

as I wrote my expose
on the benefits
of abusing Adam.

Why don't you sew me a cushion for this bench?

"Why don't you sew me a cushion for this bench?"
Versace said.

What are you,
the
actual <u>Queen</u>
now?

"I guess,"
I said.
"I used to sew."

How about,
I sew your head
into
your fucking arse?

How about that??

Days.

It's been **days**.

Or weeks?

Months?

I don't know how long.

How long,
since you haven't
so much as

looked

my way.

Versace, apparently, has grown tired of my antics and has minimised all conversations to the

occasional hello

or

have you walked Gucci yet.

WEEKS OF SILENCE,

and
now
this??

I went home that night.
I went on Amazon Prime Now.

And ordered
the top-of-the-range,
Singer sewing machine,
complete with reams of cotton,
yards of bamboo rayon jersey knit fabric in black,
reels of pattern paper,
reels of muslin cloth,
and everything else
a seamstress might use
to clothe the five thousand.

"TA DA!!"

I said, showing off my new,
hand-made skirt
to Versace.

Courtesy of Google, Pinterest and YouTube combined

I twirled around and around, stopping only to strike a Vogue-esque pose.

"What do you think?"
I said,
squealing and bopping up and down.

He barely looked up.

That fucking music again.

"It's g-r-e-a-t babe,"
he said,

in the **most**

patronising voice
known to womankind.

"Did you make that?"
He said.

"YEP!
What do you think?"

His eyes were locked on the computer screen.

"Isn't it a little big for you?"

I pinched the waistband.
It forgave an extra inch or so.

"No,"
I said.
"That's how I designed it."

LOOK I MADE SOME DOG'S CLOTHES!!!

LOOK I MADE SOME DOG'S CLOTHES!!!

LOOK I MADE SOME DOG'S CLOTHES!!!

Just to recap:

1. The 21 days are up.
And then some.

Officially divorced Charlie

2. Have been stockpiling Adam from the black market.

And self-dosing heavily

3. Have discovered super-human powers within.

Includes ability to create designer clothing items from scratch in matter of hours

Includes ability to remain awake and alert for days on end

4. Have barely looked at or conversed with Versace.

Who continues to ignore my existence

5. Consistently crying self to sleep in the bedroom while Versace 'makes music' in the other room.

Pretty much winning all around

ETHAN!!"
I yelled to the other room,

"I CAN MAKE D-O-G'S CLOTHES!!"

"That's nice, honey,"
he said, not looking up from his keypad.

So that's what I did.

I started making dog's clothes.

Meeting with my therapist

"When you picture 'happiness' in your future, what do you see?"
Dr Hooberkoff said.

I picked at the soggy tissue in my hands.

"I don't know."
I said.

Sympathetic face.

"Okay, let's start with something different…

When do you last remember being happy?

Tell me about that time."

I haven't got a clue.

The day I was conceived?

"Umm,

maybe like

four or five years ago

at the start of my last relationship?"

Epiphany face.

"Ah! **Tell me more** about that time,"
he said.

I used to like watching TV.

And cuddling on the sofa.

Even though my ex didn't like it one bit.

"Watching a movie on the sofa?
I was happy doing that."

Where are we going with this face.

"Oh… kay,"
he said.

"So…
would you say…
 that being happy,

to you,

involves being in a relationship?"

"I guess so."

Eureka, we found it face.

I sniffed into my already soaked tissue, breaking it into pieces across my face.

Dr Hooberkoff passed me another tissue from the box on the table next to him.

Why does he always keep the tissues next to him??

It's not like he's ever using them.

Cheap bastard.

"Thank you," I said, taking the tissue from his hand.

"You know, Dheep,"
he said, clasping his hands together across his stomach.

"There's nothing wrong with wanting to be married, with children, someday."

I looked at his wedding finger.

I don't see a ring on your finger, my friend.

"I didn't think anyone wanted that in this city,"
I said accusingly, staring at his absent ring.

Uncomfortable face.
"Well,"
he said, fumbling over his words.
"I'm sure **not everyone** feels that way, but there will be some people who … do… want that… you know?"

He began shuffling in his seat.

Let me guess.

"We're out of time."

The shitt-ith hath hitt-ith the fan… ith

It's the day before Thanksgiving and my boss has just called me into the office.

"Dheep,
this is the
second time
you have not made it
into the office
on time,"
My boss, Joan, said.

Fuck.

"<u>You were three hours late to work today!</u>
Is there something wrong?"
she said.

I haven't got a fucking clue.

"I'm sorry,"
I said.

"I'm on this new medication

and not only can I not sleep on it,
but I seem to
blackout
for hours
on end."

I haven't got a fucking clue.

She crossed her arms and eyed me suspiciously.

"Two weeks,"
she said.

"Get it sorted."

Just to recap:

1. Have obtained a legal prescription of Adam.

And self-dosing heavily

2. Have met with Satan himself.
AKA my psychiatrist.

Who has force-fed me a worryingly high dose of anti-depressants

And who is about as useful as <u>a honeycomb teaspoon</u>

3. Have spent 24 hours of each day fizzing like a Cola bottle that fell out of the shopping cart and rolled several blocks down the street.

On a good day

4. In that time, have alternated between:

sleeping all day,
wanting to vom
and
lying on the sofa for hours on end,
staring up at the sky
and wondering

why the fuck is this my life.

5. Consequently, <u>Versace</u> has perfected the art of pretending I am no longer in the room.

Especially when I am in the room

Pretty much
winning all around.

Back to Thanksgiving

Have just overdosed on

Adam,
coffee
and
cigarettes.

Am lying on the floor in the bathroom wondering

why the fuck is this my life.

Have been throwing up bile for

five hours now.

While Versace looks on, in the next room

and pretends I am no longer alive.

To any outsider,

our relationship
is like watching

a train crash
in slow motion.

And our train is on fire.

Next to a nuclear power plant.

Being sick in the bathroom for five hours while Versace looks on

He's playing that fucking music again.

Arsehole.

I grabbed the edge of the bath and tried to pull myself closer to the sink.

You can do it.

Dizzy.

I touched the basin of the sink and felt for the rim.

Slowly now.

Get up.

Do it.

I rolled myself out of the tub and onto the floor.

Splayed.

Up at the ceiling.

Stomach pains.

I have no-one.

No-one cares.

Two hours ago, Versace knocked on the door.

"Is everything okay in there?"

"No,"
I said.

"I've been sick for the past three hours. Non-stop."

"Okay,"
He said.

"I'll get you some water."

He knocked again one hour later.

"Is everything okay in there?"
he said.

"No,"

I said.

"I've been sick for the past four hours. **Non-stop.**"

"Okay,"
He said.

"I've left a glass of water outside the door for you."

My tears dried up, hours ago.

It's time to say goodbye.

I dragged CC across the floor,
opened her up
and found the little baggy.

Six left.

I took two,
and swallowed them dry.

Twenty days to go.

Fuck.

I threw the rest back in CC and crawled over to the door.

I lay on the floor, reached up and pulled at the handle.

Gucci.

Fuck.

Why do I always forget about him?

"Mama's going away now,"
I said, trying to reach for a kiss.

His eyes pleaded me not to go.

Don't fucking do that to me.

"I'll be back for you,"
I said, almost crying.

"I promise."

Gucci shifted his butt around until he had his back to me.

FFS Gucci.

Not now.

"Come here you monster."

I dragged him towards me and into my arms.
I fell backward.

Fuck.

The door closed.

Gucci nestled himself into my armpit, with his face over my shoulder,
watching me.

Please don't.

My body whistled through muffled tears.

I kissed his face.

"Be good for mama,"
I said,
staring up at the ceiling.
"Be… good…"

I reached up behind me.
CC.

Just two more.

I swallowed.

I lay there some more.

Eventually, I reached up for the edge of the bath and perched myself on the edge.

You can do it.

Nausea flooded my body.

Quick.

I stumbled over to the toilet cistern and lifted up the lid

Fuck.

Here it goes again.

Sit back down.

Oh fuck.

I hate my life.

I get up.

Use the bowl.

Almost.

Fuck.

Here it goes again.

Sit back down.

PLEASE LET THIS FUCKING BE IT.

There can't be anything left.

Water water water.

Too far.

On my knees.

Praying.

Please no more??

I get up.

Use the bowl.

And again.

Fuck.

Here it goes again.

I scream.

I cry.

I pray for help.

No-one cares.

No-one came.

Tired,
I rest my head,
on the bowl.

Finish now.

Please.

I fell back to the floor and closed my eyes.

It was a highly dramatic end to an intensely dramatic life.

How did I make it all the way to the bed?

As I lay there on the bed, I felt the blood drain from my fingers,

and then
my hands,
my arms,
my chest.

It's over.

Isn't it.

Cold.

Everything feels cold.

I can't move.

I can't speak.

Gucci pricked up his ears,
and climbed onto my stomach,
shivering.

He's never done that before.

He's staring at an empty space on the wall.

Heart.

Slowing down.

I don't see what he's staring at.

"Ethan?"
I whisper.

There.

My late grandmother,
grandfather,
uncle
and two cousins

standing
next to
our bed.

I'm not ready.

"Ethan?"
I whisper.

"Ethan?"

Fucking music.

He'll never hear me.

I'm too cold to cry.

I don't want to die.

I don't want to die.

"I SAID!"

"I DON'T WANT TO DIE."

Living to see another day

A funny thing happens when facing death's door.

You start making decisions.

And writing lists.

Lots of lists.

It wasn't the first time I'd faced death's door and I was sure it wouldn't be the last.
But something was very different about this time.

I didn't want to die.

That much became apparent.

"I've decided to quit my job,"

I told Dr Hooberkoff.

"Right," he said, "well that's wonderful!"

Fake smile face.

I waited.

"And do you have something else lined up, or....?"

He began rolling his hand, motioning for me to jump in.
"Well, as you know,"
I said,
"I have explored many options over the year - both internally and externally to my company..."

He began nodding.

"And nothing seems to be progressing..."

More nodding.

"So, I just decided

to quit,

and see where life takes me."

"Oh...kay..." he said.

"And any ideas on what you might want to do next?..."

"Not really,"
I said.

Silence.

"I was thinking I might open up a dog clothing business,"
I said.

Silence.

"I've started prototyping some ideas and putting them on Instagram…
just 2 weeks in, I have over 4,000 followers."

Silence.

"Well, that's
great,"
he said.

I'm going to quit my job

1. Have spoken to psychiatrist
AKA The devil

Who has informed me that I am not suited to a 9-5 job, and certainly not the 6.30-5.30 job I am currently in.

And perhaps I should consider a less stressful job, that commences after 10.30am.

2. Have spoken to HR
AKA The devil's advocate

Who advised my job is at risk if I don't turn things around.

3. Have spoken to my boss, Joan

Who advised my job is at risk if I don't turn things around.

So that's done then.

My finger is hovering

over the
resignation
button.

**Yes,
there is
an actual
'resignation'
button.**

On the intranet,
on the home page.

Employee Services:
Submit resignation.
(Button)

My finger is on the button.

Ring ring, ring ring, ring ring.

Phone call:
Versace.

"Hello?"

Muffled voices.

I got up from my seat and ducked into an empty meeting room.

"Hello?" I said again.

The sound of a voice crying.

"Ethan?"

"Ethan, is that you??
What's wrong??"

"I'm sorry!"

He exclaimed.

He got fired.

No explanation.

That's it.

I'm not going to quit my job

I'm not going to quit my job.

How can I?

We can't both be homeless.

Can we?

Week One

"Honey, I'm home!"

I said, listening out for life.

He hasn't moved since I left.

Nearly 24 hours ago.

"Does Gucci need his walkies??"
I said,
more to Gucci,
than to Versace.

"Errr...
Yes..."
He said, eyes glued on the screen.

Gucci was innocently nestled amongst a heap of unopened mail and bills.

"Shall I take him, then?"
I asked.

"Ohhh
yes,
if you don't mind...
that'd be

great."

Eyes still glued to the screen.

"Okay then…
C'mon Gucci…"

Week three

"Hi, we're home."

We just got back from our walk.

He hasn't moved since we left.

"C'mon Gucci…
dinner time"
I said,
filling up his bowl.

Where do we start?

Kitchen.

I cleared last night's leftovers from the kitchen counter and wiped the surfaces.
Wash the dishes.

What is all this shit??

He's been building something again.

God only knows what.

I'm just going to
pretend
I didn't see
that massive
makeshift
cardboard
DOOR
standing
upright
in the centre
of the room.

Just work away.

Quietly.

I worked around the tools, wires, bits of foam and cardboard scattered all over the floor or scotch-taped to the walls.

"I'm building a recording studio,"
he said.

He was sat
in the centre of the room,
opposite the door,
holding a scalpel.

Like someone might enter

through the door

at any minute.

"That's nice honey,"
I said, without looking up.

I collected ten empty Pepsi cans from various hiding places around the apartment.

Especially love the half empty one next to the toilet.
In between the scented candles.

Nice touch.

"What do you think?"
He said.

I regrettably made eye contact

with the door.

"What are you going to do with it, exactly?"
I asked.

"It's going to be the door to my recording studio."

He said,
as if it were

the most normal
thing
in the world.

He lifted up the cardboard door, sandwiched with foam and wrapped in bedsheets.
And carried it to the entrance to the bathroom to where I was stood.

"It's going to be…
right…
here…"

He held it over the opening from the lounge to the hallway.

The hallway
that led to
the bathroom
and the bedroom
which was
no larger

than his bedroom closet.

"Why here?"
I said.

"Because!!"
He said.

His tone
implying
I was
a complete moron
for even asking.

"It has the best acoustics!"
He said, smirking to himself.

He began sizing the monstrosity up against the opening, securing it with more scotch tape.

"That's nice honey,"
I said.

Week five

"Hi, we're home."

We just got back from our walk.

He hasn't moved since we left.

"C'mon Gucci…
dinner time"
I said,
filling up his bowl.

Sofa.

I re-made the sofa, ironing out the creases in the blankets with my hands and replacing the cushions, one by one.

Hoover.

I took the hoover out from the closet and whipped it around the apartment,
careful to avoid the masses of tools, wires and buttons scattered in neat piles around the room.

Ash trays.

I cleaned out all of the ash trays and wiped them over.
Don't forget the ones outside.

Clothes.

I moved around the apartment, collecting any stray items of clothing that had escaped from the closet and collapsed across the furniture and the floors.

What does he do,

host a fashion show every day, while I'm at work??

Dishes.

I cleared away all the plates, cans and left-out takeout boxes.

Time for bed.

"Goodnight, Ethan,"
I said, wearily as I passed his desk.

Still hasn't moved.

I scooped up Gucci and took him with me to the bedroom.

"Goodnight,"
Versace said, as I closed the bedroom door.

I climbed under the covers, with Gucci under my arm and fell asleep.

In the mornings

I fucking hate my life.

I tiptoed around Gucci,
careful not to wake him.

Let him sleep.

Half asleep,
I took the recommended dose of Adam,
and a little extra.
And some anti-depressants.

I need coffee.
I need a cigarette.

Into the next room.

Still hasn't moved.

Hunched over the keyboard,
drooling.

I hoisted his arm around my neck, and lifted.

To the couch.

"Mehmehmorrneh..."

Inaudible.

I stretched him across the length of the sofa and covered him with the leopard blanket.

Gucci.

I skulked back to the bedroom and lifted Gucci from his resting place, without disrupting his curled position.
I took him over to the sofa and replaced him under Versace's arm, in the same sleeping position.

Coffee.
Cigarette.

GUCCI, GET BACK TO

BED!!

Silly monster.

Try that again.

Coffee.
Cigarette.
Shower.
Work.

Meh.

Week seven

"It's Christmas Day tomorrow?"
Versace said.

He startled me.

I'm in the kitchen, scrambling eggs.
He's sat at his desk.
I have my back to him.

Still hasn't moved.

"Yes," I said.

I stopped momentarily,
and stared ahead.

Keep scrambling.

"Why aren't you spending it with your family?"
he said.

A bubble,
in my throat.

Breathe.

"The flights were too expensive," I said.

I won't leave you.

Keep scrambling.

Breathe.

"Aren't you going to miss your family?"
he asked.

I stopped again.

"Not really,"
I said.

"I hardly ever spend the holidays with them anymore."

I love you.

Tears,
in my throat.

Breathe.

"Didn't you want to spend it with your family?"
I asked.

Silence.

"No,"
he said.

I poured some eggs onto two plates and left a portion in the pan.

**Versace.
Me
And Gucci.**

I chopped an avocado and added half to each plate.
I added some spinach leaves.
And tomatoes.

Then
I doused his plate
with a shit load of Ramen noodles.

I brought Versace's plate to him, along with a can of Pepsi, leaving them both on his desk.

Without drawing attention.

I took my meal across the room to the dining table and tucked in.

He's found the Pepsi…

He's drinking the Pepsi…

SHIT!

He's looking over!

Head down.

Back to the Pepsi…

Has he seen it yet?

He's seen it.

Go on, Ethan…

take a bite…

just one mouthful…

it's been days…

Shit! Shit!

Head down!

Mmmmmm mmmmmm…

what **lovely** food this is…

I'm just
so

engrossed

in my food…

mmmmmm…

Just
eat
the damn food
Versace.

He's doing something alright…

He's just looking at it…
===

Just fucking eat it will you already.

This is actually pretty good…

I have to say…

Go me.

Wait….

Is that…

Holy fuck, it's a Christmas miracle.

He's

eating.

A welcomed change from the usual,

"You'd think you'd get the hint by now…
and stop making these breakfasts every day…"

Which I curtly reply with:

"I exist just to annoy you.

But thanks very much, Ethan…
I'll just go collect my wings now…"

Oh, shit,
he's coming over.

Keep your head down…

He's put his plate by the sink behind me…

He's walking over to the balcony…

I savoured and deliberated every remaining morsel, before joining him.

Don't check his plate…

Don't draw attention.

I went back **a good hour later** to

casually

wash the dishes.

RESULT!!!

He ate the noodles.

Christmas Day

It's Christmas day, 7pm, to be precise.

Versace has just told me to

"close my eyes"

for my

"surprise."

Now, yesterday evening, also around 7pm, he told me a very similar thing...
We were discussing gifts and I was just

triple confirming

that we

still weren't

exchanging gifts.

Just to be sure.

"Actually,"

he said.

"Actually,
I have a surprise for you...

I did get you something...

And would you like it now...

because I think you're

really going to like it...

I mean

REALLY

going to like it…"

OMFD.

He's got me
an engagement ring,
hasn't he.

Fuck.

And I haven't fucking got him anything.

So much for "NO GIFTS".

Now,
it's Christmas Eve,
at 7
fucking
pm,

and

NOW

I'm going to have to go out and get him

A FECKING CHRISTMAS PRESENT.

"Err… save it for tomorrow please…
I just have to go and run some errands… BYE…"

Christmas Day

It's Christmas day, 7pm, to be precise.

Versace has just told me to

"close my eyes"

for my

"surprise."

My eyes are fully closed.

"Yes, they are fully closed."

I hear him flapping around the room…

He's moving stuff around, I think?...

What is he doing??

I can hear music.

Interesting choice of music Versace.

Techno.

Something he's made...

himself...

Moving...

Dragging...

Something...

"OKAY, OPEN YOUR EYES!!!"

NOTHING could have prepared me for what happened next.

Versace.

Kneeling.

On the floor…

Holding…

a flashing
disco ball…

and get this…

as smoke

from a smoke machine

engulfs

the entire room

with smoke.

A smoke machine.

Disco ball.

And fucking techno music playing.

It's
a
70s
throwback
in our living room.

"I'm confused?..."

I said.

"Isn't it amazing??"

he said.

Isn't what amazing??

I waited.

And then I waited some more.

…

And some more.

That was fucking it.

"I'm going to bed."

Things could be worse

That was so nice of him to lend me his prized holdall.

I might keep it.

I'm about to crack open the wine and Netflix.

Yawn.

Let me just unpack this thing first…
or I'll never do it…

Done.

Did I forget something?

A piece of paper.

What's that then.

Nosey, I unfolded the paper.

STATE OF NEW YORK CRIMINAL COURT ORDER OF PROTECTION

Sorry, order of what now.

STATE OF NEW YORK
CRIMINAL COURT
ORDER OF PROTECTION

Ethan's name?

And who's that?

KATHERINE
WHO NOW??

STATE OF NEW YORK
CRIMINAL COURT
ORDER OF PROTECTION

Katherine Tesla,
DEFENDANT
V
Ethan Banner,
PLAINTIFF

WHO THA FUCK IS THIS BASIC BITCH!!!

From 3 years ago??

WHAT IS THIS???

I flipped open my Mac and started googling.

Google, you fucking better not let me down now.

A criminal proceeding??

For assault and/or harassment??

WHAT THA FUCK IS THIS SHIT???

My mind raced back to every physical encounter we'd had over the course of the year.

Not much tbh.

Violence?

Aggression??

Not really…

Well there was that one time…?

NO,
CAN'T BE.

I dismissed the thought from my mind
and folded up the piece of paper,
hiding it in my undie drawer.

NONSENSE. UTTER NONSENSE.

A month later

He's a fucking idiot
I hate him.

"WHAT DO YOU MEAN, YOU ONLY GET THE WORST OF ME???"

"I MEAN…"
he said.
"ONLY I

HAVE TO SEE
ALL THIS."

He's pointing to my face.

He's making fun of my disease.

He's a fucking idiot
I hate him.

A few hours later

I'm on the balcony.

I have been crying over four hours.

While he sleeps soundly.

In the next room.

He doesn't love me.

Our whole entire relationship has been a lie.

The next day.

"WHAT THA FUCK IS THIS."

I thrust the piece of paper at him, with the order of protection on it.

The biggest load of bullshit answer, ever invented, in the history of the world, ever.

Packing my bags.

"I'm leaving you forever."

GOODBYE VERSACE ETHAN BANNER.

For good.

NEXT IN THE SERIES:

A NEW YORK KIND OF LOVE, VOLUME 2

A NEW YORK KIND OF LOVE, VOLUME 3

A NEW YORK KIND OF LOVE, VOLUME 4

A NEW YORK KIND OF LOVE, VOLUME 5

A NEW YORK KIND OF LOVE, VOLUME 6

A NEW YORK KIND OF LOVE, VOLUME 7

A NEW YORK KIND OF LOVE, VOLUME 8

All books in the series are available on Amazon worldwide.

You've finished read volume one of *A New York Kind Of Love*. You can find the rest of my books at Amazon.com/author/dheep.

Please enjoy an extract from my prequel memoir series On the Fence on the next page…

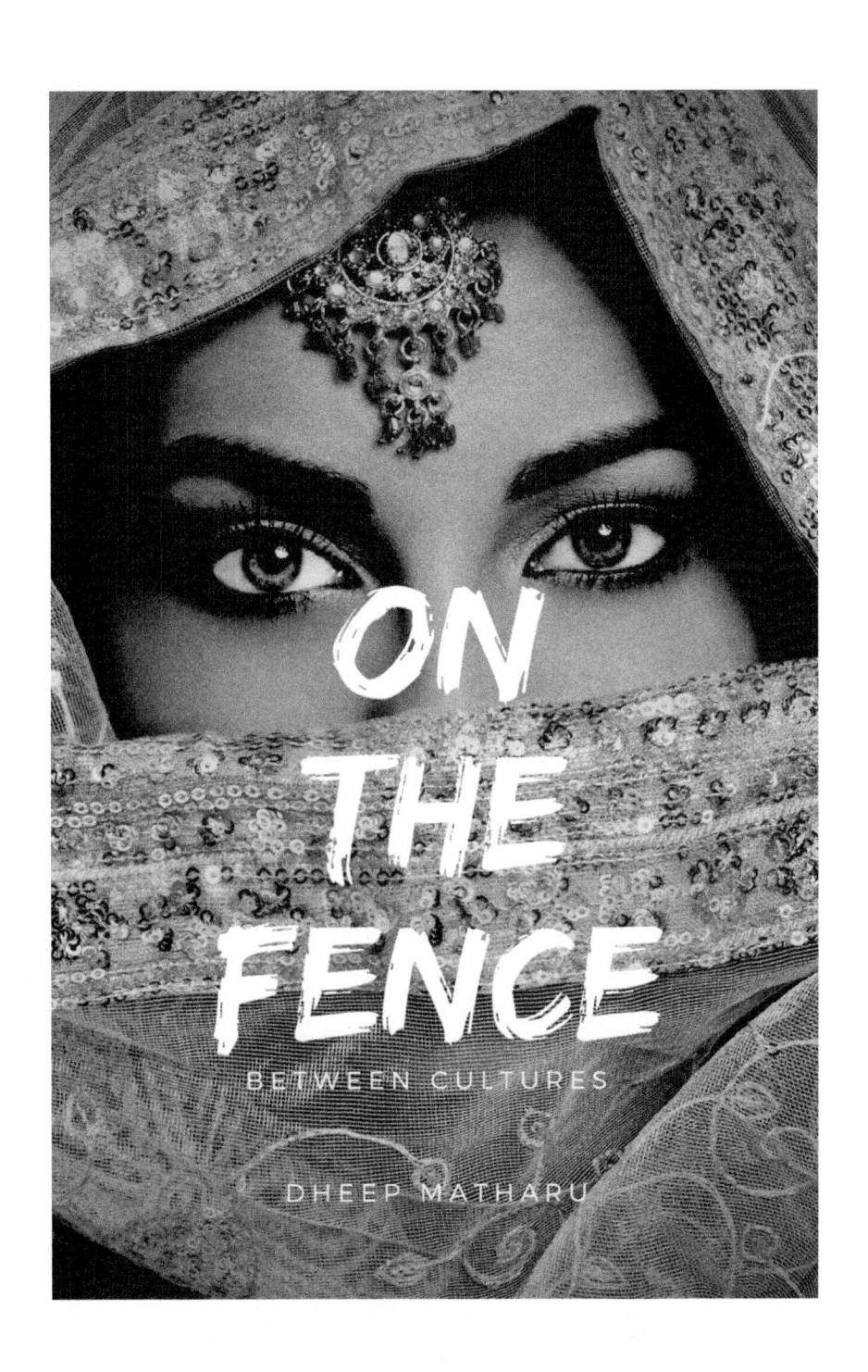

ON THE FENCE

BETWEEN CULTURES

DHEEP MATHARU

ON THE FENCE

Episode One Extract

A teen memoir about booze, drugs, parties and growing up in 90s England

Episode One: A Paki

Running

The concrete was uncomfortable.
Its crystals tore at my feet as I tried to run away.

This hurts.

The wind was seething,
spitting and cutting
into my cheeks,
stinging my eyes.

I'm not going back.

Never again.

I'll die out here
first,
before I step
one foot
back in there.

I swallowed hard

and kept running
until

faceplant.

Great.

"Dheep!"

I hear Emma,
calling my name.

🎀 Meet Emma 🎀

Emma
is the
Barbie doll
my Grandma
cut into pieces

because she doesn't want us to have daughters, later in life.

She's also my best friend.

She legit
stepped out of a magazine,
where the models all hang out,
with their other
hot friends.

Except
I'm not hot.

<u>I'm about</u>
<u>as different to Emma</u>
<u>as black is to white.</u>

Her hair is the literal colour of straw, except for a few stripes of white scattered about, which I helped her colour with them new at-home brush highlight kits by Maybelline.

Because we're worth it.

Her eyes are shards of caramel and olive.

But
if anyone asks
they're green.

If she ever had a blemish I would shoot myself in the face.

Because it never happened.

She is beautiful.

Even her cheeks grew with their own dusty pink blush.

Barbie.

Barbie.

Back to the party

The wind is shrieking around me, through my ears.

"Take me.
I'm ready.
Take me."

I whispered into the tarmac.

"Dheep!
<u>What the fuck
are you doing?!"</u>

Emma.

"Just leave me.

*It's
my
time..."*

I whined,

batting her feet away.

"Dheep! Get the fuck off that floor!!

NOW!!!"

Even her feet are pretty.

"No," I cried. "I'm not going back there…"

"Fine,"
Emma said

and sat down, legs crossed and handed me the bottle.

The next morning

The next morning
I woke.

Hair stuck
to my face.

Disgusting.

Where am I?
What time is it??

I peeled myself up from the sofa.

Bad move.

My brain
vibrating
my skull.

Ouch

isn't
even
the
word.

I rolled down my dress and reviewed the scene.

Bodies.

Everywhere.

On the sofas,
wrapped in sheets
or huddled on the floors.

One sleeping on the stairs.

Who sleeps on the stairs??

Beer cans.
WKD bottles.
And some carpet,
once cream,
now
a masterpiece
Pollock
would be proud
to call his own.

Which one is Emma???

MATT.

SHE'S WITH MATT!!

But where…

"Emma.."
I whispered through the door as I gently knocked.

"Em-ma.."

Shuffles and murmurs
on the other side.

Eventually Emma appeared through the crack in the door.

"Mweh," she said.

"I've gotta head home." I said.
"You coming?"

"One sec.."

Last night

What is it
about the words
'last night'
that never
end well.

They should remove those words from our vocabulary.

Last night.

Last night.

Ugh.

Last night.

Last night I was a twat.

Ugh.

Last night

should be wiped
from my memory.

Except James.

James
should never be wiped
from anyone's
memory.

James.

James.

James makes Jack Ryder look ugly.

If that weren't sacrilege.

Last night
he spoke to me
for exactly three seconds.

"It's strong," James said.

To me.
He said to me.
About the wine.

Or whatever we were drinking.

I giggled,
rolled my hair to my left side,
leant back on the counter
and gently hitched up
the corner of my dress,
to reveal more thigh.

"Yeah.
It is strong,"
I said,
stretching my knee and tapping my toes against the floor.

I looked at him
and pouted
though my smile.

He didn't notice.

And then Emma dragged me away.

"I LOVE THIS SONG!!!" Emma squealed.

Except
she doesn't squeal,
she chirps.
The way Barbie chirps
if she were meant to talk.

This is my chance,

I thought,

for James to notice me.

Dancing sexy looks way better in the videos.
You'd think it would be easy sexy dancing to Craig David and his 7 days

but oh no.

I'm dancing with an invisible hula hoop.

Because this is sexy, isn't it.

You've finished read episode one of *On the Fence*. You can find the rest of the book series at Amazon.com/author/dheep.

As a special thank you gift, keep reading to receive episode one for free upon joining my newsletter!

AUTHOR NOTES

Welcome to my author notes! This is where I reflect back on this book and share my thoughts about it. It's also where I get a chance to talk to you more directly.

My story is still ongoing, so I'll be working on the next instalments soon, writing from my hometown in Kent, England. If you haven't seen it already, I've another memoir book series which I also write called, "On the Fence". It's the prequel to this series. You can find it on Amazon. It's written in a similar writing style and you can expect the same gritty honesty!

At the moment I'm working on writing a book about spirituality on how to trust your inner (God) voice. It's still a working draft so it's not out yet. I'd love you to join my advanced reader team for the pre-launch of all my upcoming books where I give you access to free copies of my books before they go on sale. Please send me an email if you would like to join the team or join my closed Facebook group, both of which you can find at the end of this book.

Volume one was by far my favourite in the series. I had so much fun writing it and re-living the "hot mess" lifestyle of this ex-New Yorker! It's all downhill from here!

I thoroughly hope you've enjoyed reading this book and I look forward to seeing you in the next one!

With gratitude,
Dheep

QUICK FAVOUR

I'm wondering, are you enjoying this book series? First of all, thank you for reading my book! May I ask a quick favour?

Will you take a moment to leave an honest review for this book series on Amazon? Reviews are the BEST way to help others purchase the book series and I truly appreciate it.

You can go to the relevant link below and write your thoughts or leave a product review on Amazon. I appreciate you!

DHEEPMATHARU.COM/ANYKOLREVIEW

THANK YOU GIFT

I want to say thank you! To say thank you for leaving a review, I would like to give you a free gift!

Sign up to my newsletter using the link below and you will receive a FREE copy of the first book in my memoir series *On the Fence*, the prequel series to *A New York Kind of Love*.

On the Fence, a modern-day, tell-it-like-it-is teen memoir series will have your sides splitting!

I appreciate you!

DHEEPMATHARU.COM/OTFFREE

CONTACT THE AUTHOR

I love connecting with you and sharing stories. Please write to me if this book series has impacted you in any way. I love to hear from you!

To be the first to know when the next volume of the series is out and any other author related goodies by signing up to my newsletter. I love sharing with you!

I've included all my details on the next page so please write to me, follow me, sign up to my newsletter and advanced reader team. Phew!

God bless you and thank you again for sharing this journey with me.

Amen.

Dheep Matharu

New Age Christian Spiritualist and Bestselling Author of A New York Kind of Love

Join my newsletter and receive special offers, new release details, and a welcome gift delivered right to your inbox.

- ✉ dheep.writer@gmail.com
- f Dheep Uncensored
- ⓘ @DheepUncensored
- ♥ dheepmatharu.com
- 📰 dheepmatharu.com/newsletter
- ★ dheepmatharu.com/art (Advanced Reader Team)

If you've been affected by addiction or mental health, you can reach out to Addaction or The Samaritans.

You can find them on www.addaction.org.uk or www.samaritans.org, respectively.

Printed in Great Britain
by Amazon